Through Persecution to Freedom

Uganda: A Land of Tragedy and Hope

By
Steven Kaweesa

Compiled and written by
Sheryl Gorman

1st Books - rev. 04/03/03

DEDICATION

I dedicate this book to
Ron and Shirley DeVore.

To this wonderful man and woman
of God, I humbly dedicate this work
to their great service in Uganda
and the whole of Africa.

- Stephen Kaweesa

Table of Contents

IN APPRECIATION

❖ Thank you to all of my children who have given me such a great encouragement: Rachel, Phillip, Margaret, Lillian, Isaac, Andrew and Richard. Thank you!

❖ Thank you to my pastors, Ron Devore and Steven Mayanja. You have stood with me all these years, in times of joy and times of pain. Thank you.

❖ Thank you, Pastor Jeff, for encouraging me to write this book. And, Sheryl, for your many hours. It's a work well done.

❖ Thanks, Brother Douglas, for giving your time to help make the tape recordings, and for making sure that every tape came out good for this book.

❖ Thanks to all of those who came to proofread the book, word after word: Rob, Shellie, Kent, Laurie, David and Julie. It's a work well done.

❖ Thank you, Brother Andrew, with Open Doors ministry, for helping to support me during the early years of my ministry with $30 per month. Also, I was one of those you sent a bicycle. God bless you.

❖ Thank you, Reinhard Bonnke. I met you in 1983 in Amsterdam. Your coming to Uganda has been a great encouragement to us. We are now going through revival. Thank you for standing with us!

❖ Thank you, Brother Billy Graham, for making it possible for me to attend the World Conference about Evangelism in Amsterdam in 1983. Although I was young at the time, I have now reached many for Christ. Thank you.

❖ Thank you, T.L. Osborn, for your encouragement to our country. You came even during the difficult years of war. Great things are now happening in Uganda. God bless.

❖ Thanks, Morris Cerrulo. In 1978 you invited me to a minister's conference in Kenya, and then in 1979, you invited me to California for training. My air ticket was stolen, but they didn't steal Jesus from me! Thank you for standing with us in Uganda!

~ Introduction ~

Dear Reader,

With great enthusiasm and expectation I present this book to you. With enthusiasm, because it has been a joy and a privilege to work on Pastor Kaweesa's project. With expectation, because I believe that as you read these amazing stories of God's love, power and faithfulness, you will be greatly encouraged.

Some of you may know and appreciate "Ugandan English". Perhaps you know Pastor Kaweesa or have been to Africa. I want to let you know that every effort has been made to preserve the flavor and speaking style of Pastor Kaweesa as he shares with you these inspiring stories of God's power. Some grammatical rules have been forfeited in order to allow you to savor and enjoy his testimony.

I have now learned some things in my life, and one of those "nuggets" of truth that I have been blessed to find is this: Not every wrapper does the contents justice. Allow me to explain.

As a child, your first bicycle may have come to you in a large, bulky, rather plain brown box. It wasn't until you opened that box that you discovered with sheer delight the contents. Perhaps the bicycle was bright red with chrome fenders, and was equipped just the way you wanted.

Or consider this. Quite possibly you have visited one of those homemade, bake-it-from-scratch bakeries where as you walk through the door the mouth-watering aroma begs you to considering buying one of everything! But, by the time you make your way to the counter, you have regained control and manage to order only a few more things than you actually went in for. Your order is placed into a plain paper sack, disguising the true value of your treasure, and off you go.

Well, I have said all that to say this. Pastor Kaweesa is one of those nearly hidden treasures. I have come to realize that residing within this very kind and humble man is a powerhouse of God's very nature. Through Pastor Kaweesa flows the power of Jesus Christ that sets captives free, heals the sick, and brings salvation and hope.

We have been trained in our society to be stimulated by sight. Everywhere we look, things are calling out to us through visual aids. We are inspired to buy a certain hamburger just because we saw it drive by us on a truck a half hour earlier on the freeway. Or, we are tempted to buy a certain car because of the convincing advertisements.

And, sadly, that way of shiny thinking has carried over in to church circles today. We see the flock of God mesmerized by certain people because they are so "shiny"! And, all the while, there are dear saints and servants of the Most High God in our very midst quietly and faithfully trudging through the harvest fields filling their baskets with the precious fruit that the Master is waiting for.

I think it is going to be very interesting and refreshing when we get to heaven to find out who the "heavyweights" really were. Was it that little old grandma that reached heaven with her prayers and prayed through more than one lost soul to the throne? Or, was it one of those unseen missionaries in a foreign land that fed the hungry, clothed the naked, and brought the true light of the Gospel to those dear to God's heart?

I praise God for every great woman and man of God that is serving faithfully today. I thank God for those who are committed to the cause of Christ and refuse to give up or to grow weary until the job is finished. However, I feel to challenge each one of us to open up our eyes to see what the

Spirit of God is doing in the earth today. The Lord's eyes go to and fro throughout the earth looking for a "heart" that He can show Himself strong through and for.

Be a "chosen vessel". Be a vessel that God can pour His power and nature through. And, be blessed as you read about one such vessel of the Lord who has served and continues to serve our Lord Jesus Christ faithfully. . . . . Pastor Stephen Kaweesa!

~ Sheryl Gorman
Co-Founder and Co-Pastor
Great Round-Up Outreach Center
Ellensburg, Washington USA

~ One ~

THE TORTUROUS RULE

OF IDI AMIN

When the righteous are in authority,
the people rejoice;
But when a wicked man rules,
the people mourn.
Proverbs 29:2

Steven Kaweesa

IDI AMIN COMES TO POWER

When Idi Amin first came into power in 1971, he seemed to be a good president. However, it turned out that he was one of the worst leaders ever of Uganda. He began torturing and killing the people of our country.

After coming into power, Idi Amin soon closed the doors of the churches. Baptist churches, Pentecostal churches, Presbyterian churches, Seventh-Day Adventist churches, and many other churches were closed. Only the Catholic, Anglican and Muslim churches were allowed. Those were the churches that Idi Amin considered to be good for his people. The rest, he considered to be fake and a threat to his government.

When Idi Amin closed the churches, he not only threatened the church, he threatened almost everyone. First, were the Indians. Idi Amin said that he had had a dream, and when he awoke, he said that God had told him that all the Indians and the Whites must leave the country within ninety days. These Indians were the ones who were holding nearly all of the big businesses and assets in Kampala, the biggest city in our country.

So, all the Indians, which were numbered in the thousands, had to pack up and leave Uganda. As I have told you, they were holding the large businesses. They could not take their businesses with them. They had to leave everything behind. They left within those ninety days. Idi Amin then gave their properties to his government officials and to the Muslims, those who had helped him overthrow the previous Ugandan government.

3

~*~*~

Writer's word of warning: *Due to the graphic content, the following segment may not be suitable for children. This testimony has been included as told by Pastor Kaweesa. It includes his eyewitness account of the persecution and killing in Uganda under Idi Amin's rule.*

PRISONS, TORTURES & DEATH

That was not the end. Even the Ugandans who stayed behind experienced hard times. Idi Amin had torturing prisons. It was very, very, very terrible.

One prison that I knew well and saw those that were tortured there, was the prison where there was much broken glass on the floor. People were put there with no clothes on and barefooted. When you live in such a prison, your feet are pierced by those broken pieces of glass.

In addition, Idi Amin had men, who used all sorts of methods of torturing people, so that they may seek information. Idi Amin believed these people were fighting the government. However, most of the people that were arrested were just innocent and poor people.

Idi Amin's men had terrible weapons which they used to torture and kill. One method is that they took hammers, hammered in your head and killed you straight away. Another killing method was the firing squad.

They also had a kind of torturing method where they took a knife or similar weapon from a hot, burning stove and cut off the prisoner's ears, nose, hands, or legs. They would do that in phases. They would not cut them all off at once. Every day they would cut off something different. One day they may cut off your nose, and then another day they may cut off your hand, another day they could cut off your leg and so on. This would go on for several days. Although you are alive, you are in a very, very, terrible pain, which is extremely hard to explain.

Another method of torture, which is very difficult to mention, is that they would not feed the prisoners. They would just throw them into a room and they would have to survive from their own human waste. When a new prisoner was thrown into the room, those that had spent many days there were happy because they would have some urine to drink. This meant they could survive for a few more days. These are some of the tortures I saw during Idi Amin's rule.

Sometimes, as soldiers arrested a person, they would tie the prisoner's arms and legs very tightly, twisting them to cause severe pain. Then, soldiers would throw them into the trunk of a vehicle and drive around on terrible roads for thirty, forty, and even fifty miles. By the time they got the prisoner out of the vehicle, they were almost dead. Then soldiers would take them to one of the torturing prisons where they would begin another phase of torturing.

The following, is another type of torturing that I witnessed. Idi Amin's soldiers got hold of a man and commanded him to undress right in public, which he did. Then, they got a brick that was very heavy, the kind of brick that is used to build houses. With rope, they tied the brick to this man's private part so that it was weighing down. Four soldiers on each side of this man, with their guns pointing at him, commanded him to raise his arms up and would not let him put his arms down. The weight of the brick caused terrible pain, which is beyond description.

Idi Amin ordered the killing of many people. Soldiers threw some of the dead bodies in Namanve Forest along Jinja highway. It is about seven kilometers from Kampala. There they threw hundreds of dead bodies, hundreds of dead bodies.

~*~*~

FRUITS OF A JEALOUS RAGE

I remember a gentleman who lived not far from where I lived. He had just built himself a new home, a very nice home, and was throwing a grand party to celebrate his new home. He had invited all his friends from different walks of life to help him celebrate. Idi Amin's men were so jealous of him that they took him, tortured him and then threw him in the prison. After that, they killed him and threw him in the forest, of which I have told you.

Idi Amin had different places where he threw the dead bodies. Bodies were thrown in the place in the forest, and dead bodies were put in Lake Victoria, or in the River Nile, wherever he wanted. Forest places. Bush places. And at anytime, you could end up being killed.

This gentleman's people looked for him, but could not find him. They looked and looked and looked for him. Over ten days later, they finally went down to the forest. People knew that when you lose someone you go to that forest and look. That is the easiest place to go to look, because if you tried to go up to the prisons, then you would be dead.

When this man's family came to the forest, they found hundreds of dead bodies, dead bodies from men and ladies, young ladies, young men, all kinds of dead bodies and even dead bodies of the children. They found his dead body. And my, it was rotten and maggots covered the whole body. They brought that dead body home and they buried it.

~*~*~

TYRANNY + FEAR = DEATH

The time came when Idi Amin could trust almost no one. You could hear that all kinds of people were being murdered. Much suffering took place among Christians, as well as non-Christians. Any citizen of Uganda could be "picked". However, if you were a Muslim, and had a hat on your head, then you were very safe.

One way that people could be "picked", was because of their houses. People could be picked because of their vehicles, or the way they looked. They were picked because of their job or profession. Especially those who worked in the banks, the doctors, and the lawyers were at risk. Those people died in the thousands. I tell you, many doctors, many lawyers, and many professional people had to run away from the country. If you didn't, you knew that at any time you could be killed. Even if you wore glasses, you could be killed, or, if you wore a watch. These items were a sign that you could read and count. Any educated person could be a threat to the government.

Among the prominent killed, was the Chief Justice, Ben Kiwanuka. He was picked right from his chamber and was never seen again. Idi Amin even killed some of his own Cabinet. He arrested the Arch Bishop of the Church of Uganda. We were given the news that an accident had happened and they were dead. It was a lie. We knew it was a lie. Idi Amin was very furious. He used knives and cut off their heads. There was no safe person in Uganda during this time.

A funny thing that Idi Amin always said was, "I fear no one in this country; I fear no one in this world, except God." He lied to the whole world that he was the very friend of God! Yet, he was doing all these kinds of terrible, terrible things.

Idi Amin killed his own cabinet members and officials, as well as his own soldiers. One day as we were walking along Bombo road, a big truck went by that was loaded with Idi Amin's soldiers, crying and calling out, "If anyone can help us, please do. They are taking us to kill us."

But, no one could help. Later, we came to know that those men were from the native tribes, the Achols and the Langis.

So, those are some of the types of tortures and killings that took place during the time of Idi Amin. There were quite a different number of types of tortures. Some I have forgotten. It was terrible and one does not even want to think of the suffering and pain which took place during that time.

~*~*~

Question & Answer

Q: Pastor Kaweesa, during that time of persecution, did believers forsake their faith?

A: Yes, that's true. In fact, when the persecution became very heavy, a number of Christians in our church, as well as other churches, just closed their mouths. They did not want to be bothered again with Christ.

I remember one brother who was a Christian and was very involved in the church. When the persecution rose up, we visited his house. He said to us very openly, "Please leave me alone. I have my own life. You have your own life. I can not be a stupid, foolish person to die. I can call upon God in my heart, but I do not want you to come back to my house because they know you very well. And if they see me associating with you, you are putting me in a trouble. And they are going to kill me. I don't want to die. I have a family to raise. I want to see my children grow up with me. So, please can you leave my home?" We left his home. We knew that it was only God that could help him.

So, a great number of people like that brother forsook their faith and some of them we never saw again, even to this day. Some would have nothing to do with God in that kind of time. They believed that the best way to survive was to keep quiet.

For I am not ashamed of the
Gospel of Jesus Christ,
For it is the power of God to salvation
To everyone who believes...
Romans 1:16

~ *Two* ~

SURVIVING THE ONGOING TYRANNY

You deliver me from my enemies,
You also lift me up above those
who rise against me;
You delivered me from the violent man.
2 Samuel 22:49

Steven Kaweesa

DELIVERED FROM THE VIOLENT MAN

One incident involved a sister in the church, named Alice. Alice loved the Lord. One day as she was coming back from work men in a vehicle grabbed her and accused her of being a wife of the rebels. They took her and threw her into one of the prisons. Every day she experienced seeing prisoners taken. Each morning the soldiers came, opened the prisons, and called out one by one, "You come, you come, and you come". The soldiers then took those prisoners outside and tortured them. Daily, Alice watched this happen.

I want to explain how this sister survived. She was in that prison for several days seeing all this suffering, torture and death. Every day the Lord protected her. Every day when the soldiers came, they did not call her. The days went by, and days went by, and days went by.

However, the day finally arrived when Alice's name was called and she was picked to be one of those killed that night. The soldiers came around seven o'clock in the evening. Prisoners were taken by truck to a secret place where they were hanged, shot, tortured, or whatever. Alice was put on a big truck along with over one hundred prisoners that were also to be killed. She didn't know how they were going to be killed, but she knew that was the end of her life.

But just then, a very peculiar thing happened. As the truck was about to leave, a very, very, heavy storm came. Rain came down. And do you know what? That storm stopped the soldiers from their mission. The soldiers abandoned the truck, leaving the prisoners out in that heavy storm. The prisoners were a bit happy, because they were refreshed with the rain and got a chance of having water. After it had stopped raining, it was almost ten o'clock in the night. The soldiers came and told the prisoners that they were supposed to kill them, but instead, they took them back to the prison. The Lord had moved that night.

So another week went by and Alice survived. The prisoners had no food, they only survived on human waste. Eventually, after almost one month, the commander of that prison came and said that he was going to set some of the prisoners free. He said, "When I read your name, you leave this ground right away." He began reading the names.

Eventually, he came to this sister's name. Alice, when she heard her name, was so excited! She could not believe it. She came to the church. We had been praying for her for many, many, many days to the Almighty God. Alice was set free!

~*~*~

FAITH IN THE LAST HOUR

Two brothers were going to church in the evening at about 8 o'clock, when a vehicle came right to them. Soldiers threw these two brothers inside of that vehicle. The soldiers had guns, hand grenades and all kinds of weapons. They were driven around for a long time.

The soldiers said, "We are going to kill you. You are rebels. We know that you are rebels." Each one of these brothers had their bibles in hand, and they began witnessing to the soldiers. They told them about the love of Jesus. How Jesus forgives sin and how Jesus came to save. As they shared, the fear that was in them that they were going to die just went away. They received strength.

These two brothers looked straight into the soldier's eyes and said, "You can kill the body, but you cannot kill the spirit. You can kill me today, but I know where I am going. I am going to meet my Lord. My Lord has a wonderful place prepared for me."

Eventually, their words went deep into the hearts of these soldiers. One of them confessed, "Please forgive me, because I was once born again. But, I have backslid. You pray for us." So, the soldiers dropped the brothers off and told them, "Please run, because if you don't, some of our friends may come, and if they find you, they are not going to spare you."

~*~*~

WHAT WOULD YOU DO? (WWYD)

In one of the full-gospel churches, the people were praising, praying and worshiping the Lord when soldiers came. The church was nearly full. The soldiers surrounded the whole church and then entered the church and began shooting.

Next, they lined up every Christian. The commander said, "If you are a visitor of this church, then you leave and go. But, if you are a member of this church, you stay right here." As far as I remember, around sixty people stayed. The rest went, over two hundred.

The remaining Christians were then taken to a prison. This particular prison had a very large, wide kind of grave which was open. They were all put down in that grave, over fifteen feet down. On top of this open grave, was a very powerful light that gave out an intense kind of heat. There was not enough air anywhere. The prisoners sweat terribly. They suffered for days.

The man who had ordered their arrest was the vice president of Idi Amin. He arranged a day to kill each and every one of these prisoners. When that day came, he had gone to the east side of the country. As he was coming back, he got in a very terrible accident. That accident was in the favor of these Christians who were imprisoned. He had to be taken out of the country to be treated and he never came back to Uganda.

The prisoners were taken to another prison, which was kind of a good prison, where they were imprisoned for over forty days. Eventually, Idi Amin pardoned them and told them to never go back to that kind of a church. When we heard about that we praised the Lord! We glorified the name of the Lord!

~*~*~

TIED WITH WIRE

Another type of terrible torture I saw was this. It happened to a gentleman neighbor two blocks from where I was renting. They came to his house one night and got hold of him. They took him and tied some type of wire around his body from his legs up to his chest. They tied him so tightly that the wire went through his body. He was left that way for a week. I prayed for this man and the Lord answered my prayers.

This man was not a Christian. He had nothing to do with the Lord. However, it was a miracle. He did not die.

When the soldiers saw that he had not died, they said "You must have a long life and so we are setting you free." They untied him. He could not stand. He could not sit. They took him home to his family and his family began to care for his injuries.

~*~*~

Question & Answer

Q: How did you survive, Pastor Kaweesa? During this time of persecution, was there a time when you thought of letting your faith go? Could you tell us more of what you went through and how your faith survived?

A: Yes. There were times when I thought, "Why should I die? Why should I suffer like this? Keep quiet. Is it not better for me to wait until maybe the time will come when Idi Amin is gone?" There were times when those thoughts came to me. I thought, "I will stop the ministry. And I will stop preaching. I will be on my own."

One day when I went back home I was so scared. I had received news that a brother and sister had been taken. I had seen two men tortured by being tied tightly and put in the trunk of a car. These were big gentlemen and they would not fit in the car, so the soldiers pushed on the trunk so that they would fit. These men were taken and I never saw them again. That made me so much afraid. I didn't want to die.

But, when I went back home, I had a dream. And in this dream I saw myself in a hospital. Someone was leading me to every room. Each room had many sick people with different kinds of sicknesses, critical conditions. Some were on oxygen. I saw those that were dying. I saw people dying of cancer. I saw those who had been involved in accidents. I saw those that were being operated on and then died after the operation. I saw ladies trying to give birth, but the babies would not come out, and they died.

In my dream, we walked until we ended up to where they keep the dead bodies, which we call the mortuary. At last, the gentleman with me asked, "Are all these people dying because of you?" I answered, "No, no!" And right then I knew that this was Jesus. He instructed me to "Go back and preach My Word".

When I came out of that dream I was a bit afraid, but also encouraged. I said, "Oh, my. God, you are on my side. You know my thoughts; you know my plans, what I want to do. Lord, forgive me of my wrong thoughts and thank you."

I knelt down and repented of the fear. I then felt strength from the Lord. I took this message and shared it with my fellow ministers. We were so much encouraged that we went on.

I can do all things through
Christ who strengthens me.
Philippians 4:13

~ Three ~

THE UNDERGROUND CHURCH IN UGANDA

What then shall we say to these things?
If God is for us, who can be against us?
Romans 8:31

Steven Kaweesa

BOYHOOD MEMORIES

I did not grow up with my father and mother. I grew up with my grandmother who was very poor. Later on, I moved in with my Auntie Margaret when I was about twelve years of age. She was a born-again Christian and she loved and worshiped God. The Lord had told her that in her house she would one day raise a servant of the Lord who would preach the Word of God in many places. She did not know what kind of young man that would be, because the Lord had not given her a child of her own. When I came to her home, the Lord revealed to her that this was the child He had told her of.

From that time on, my Auntie tried her level best to see that I would come to accept Jesus Christ as my Lord. At first, I didn't take her serious or pay attention to her. I had nothing to do with God, but she did not give up. She continued praying and believing God. She took me to her church, which was just a single room in someone's home. Eventually, in 1973, I accepted Christ.

During that time, persecution had begun under Idi Amin's rule. Churches were closed. I found myself in the single room "church" praying and calling on the name of the Lord. God changed me instantly. He baptized me in His Holy Spirit. I found that God was giving me messages and words to share.

I came to greatly admire my Auntie's faith in the Lord. She loved God and had much faith even in difficult situations. When the church was closed and we were forced underground, she was never worried. One time when soldiers were going to arrest us, she declared, "The Lord is with us; God is on our side. And when God is on our side, who can be against us?" That kind of faith encouraged me when I first came to receive Jesus Christ as my personal Savior.

In 1974, at the age of sixteen, I became a pastor and was very much involved in preaching the Word of God in those very, very difficult circumstances.

~*~*~

SEEKING THE FACE OF GOD "UNDERGROUND"

The owner of the house who had the small room we were meeting in soon realized that this was the kind of church that had been closed and that his life was in danger. He told us, "Please move away from here." We thought that he was only joking, but one day he brought the police. The police threatened us and told us that they were going to kill us if we didn't move away from there.

As we continued to fellowship and were in prayer, a woman took big buckets of water and poured them on us. It was very terrible, but we were a bit happy and thankful to God, for this type of persecution was because of God.

We were forced to move our church to a nearby field and we started praying right on that field. We spent three months praying every Sunday, Wednesday and Friday nights. In this field, there was no building, nothing. We just tried to find a safe place where we could pray and call upon the name of our Lord. And what is amazing is that these Christians were not discouraged, rather they were encouraged and continued to come. And not only that, they even brought new people who got born-again in the meetings.

Then, after three months, one brother offered the garage of his house to be a church. So we started gathering in that garage. He also gave us another room that we used as a prayer room. So, in this kind of fellowship, soldiers tried to come in and break the church up a number of times. But, that did not stop us.

~*~*~

SOLDIERS SENT TO KILL US

I remember one time when the soldiers came as we were praying and calling on the name of the Lord. It was a Friday night. The soldiers said to me, "What are you doing here?"

I told them, "We are praying."

Then, they told me, "We have the authority to kill you. And we have come to kill you, but we are not going to do it." So, they left. In the morning, we found out that those same soldiers had killed ten people from the other side of the village. God had saved us from that terrible act.

~*~*~

SOLDIER'S GUN FALLS APART

Another time, the soldiers came as we were praying in the prayer room and they asked us "What are you doing here?" I told them, "We are praying". One soldier came to put us outside and shoot us, but as he was doing that, he fell on the ground. Also, his gun fell apart.

23

When the other soldiers saw what had happened to him, they ran out. When the soldier that was lying on the ground woke up, we were afraid he was going to kill us. We were a bit scared, but he just grabbed his gun and ran away. So, that night the Lord spared our lives.

~*~*~

"YOU ARE REFUSED FROM PRAYING"

Also, I remember a time when I was in town with two of my colleagues. Two men came up to us and said, "We know you are praying, and you are refused from praying. We are going to come and when we do, you are not going to like it. You are going to die. We shall shoot you right on the spot! So, be aware of that!"

I thought, "My, here we are in town. We are not in the church. And, these gentlemen know us." That made me a bit worried because I realized that we could not hide anywhere, we were known everywhere. But, inside me a voice said, "Go on, for I am with you. Nothing is going to harm you." That gave me strength to go on with the work of the Lord.

"I can tell you, my friend, that there were times when I was discouraged. We prayed and prayed. We believed that one day God was going to open up our country. We didn't know how long it would take, for Idi Amin was very powerful. Even other countries feared him. But, God had assured us that it was soon all coming to an end." - Pastor Kaweesa

~*~*~

SURPRISE "OPEN AIR" MEETINGS

We began to hold Surprise "Open Air" Meetings. We made no announcements. There was no advertisement. We just assembled ourselves at different places. When we were there, we clapped our hands. We had our Bibles. Many people became born-again and joined our church. Every night people came to pray.

The church grew as time went by. However, as our congregation grew, persecution also grew.

~*~*~

GOD'S MIRACLE PROTECTION

One Sunday evening, we had gathered over 100 people when strange men came around us. I felt in my heart that these men must be soldiers. But, we trusted the Lord and looked to Him. We knew that God was on our side. We prayed and prayed and prayed.

There was a man who had come with a camera and as the people had closed their eyes and knelt down on their knees to pray, this man was busy trying to take our pictures. But, as he tried to do that, the Holy Spirit struck him and he fell down to the ground.

After we had prayed, the time came to close the meeting. As we were doing that, this man was still deep in the Holy Spirit, crying and crying and crying. The meeting was closed but the Holy Spirit was continuing. We stayed.

After over an hour this man gave us the whole story of what he had come to do. He had come to take pictures of all the people praying who were breaking the order which the government had declared in an effort to close the church. Then, they were going to find us one by one and kill us. However, this man said, "Today, I am born again." He became a Christian and he came on our side.

~*~*~

FOOT SOLDIERS WREAK HAVOC IN THE VILLAGES

Idi Amin had foot soldiers everywhere that were looking for those that were fighting his government. There were rebels who were trying to overthrow his government.

One Friday night we had gathered to pray. After the meeting, people left to go to their homes. But, soon they came running back to tell us that soldiers had surrounded every road, every junction, and every corner. I told the people to please stay put. I assured them that the good Lord that had kept us all these many times was even now going to keep us. We prayed and prayed and prayed.

What is very amazing is that through the night soldiers went from house to house searching. The soldiers seized a number of men who never came back again. Soldiers went to the house on the left of us, to the right of us, all around us. But, in the house where we had gathered, no single soldier came in that place. We knew that God had protected us. Such happenings took place a number of times.

~*~*~

SISTERS HIDE IN BUSHES

Sometimes we prayed outside on the hill, even in the nighttime. One night as two sisters were coming to climb this hill, men came in a vehicle to try to take these ladies. They escaped and hid along the side of the road in the bushes. The men came right to where they were and looked around and looked around for these ladies. What is very amazing is that the men never saw our sisters. God spared them that night.

They stayed there for awhile even after the soldiers left because they were so afraid. They thought that maybe the soldiers were still hiding somewhere. Later, they came and gave us the testimony. That night we were very happy and very thankful to the Lord.

~*~*~

SOLDIER'S EYES ARE BLINDED

We used various places to pray at night. One place was near Lake Victoria in a bushy area. We would pray there all night. On one such night, we saw soldiers coming. We did not know how they knew we were down there praying, but we thought that perhaps some people from that village had told them.

A line of about fifteen soldiers came toward us. We could not run. We knew we were in trouble. Each one of us was praying quietly right inside of our hearts. We prayed and prayed and prayed. I said, "Lord, blind their eyes just like you blinded the eyes of the men who came to capture the prophet Elisha." I prayed that prayer time after time, time after time.

The soldiers came and passed right by where we were sitting. They looked around. They spent almost two hours looking. God blinded their eyes. After they had failed to see us, they left.

God spared us that night. We were very thankful for what God had done for us.

Another time, about ten of us had gathered to pray. We had put benches together and were under the benches praying. The soldiers came right in to that place. As the soldiers sat on the benches, we were right under them!

They did not take apart the benches. Had they done that, they would have spotted us, and right now, I would be dead. We were right there. We heard them speaking. But the Lord God protected us that night.

~*~*~

"IT SHALL NOT COME NIGH YOU"

One night, soldiers surrounded my home. They went to the houses around my house and took men. In the morning, the wives of those men were weeping and crying and they told how their husbands had been taken. They were taken and never seen again.

The good Lord had protected me again. Those kinds of miracles of protection took place during the time of Idi Amin many times. I thank God so much that He can protect His people in such a great manner like that.

~*~*~

IN CHAINS, YET FREE IN CHRIST

One time as we were praying and praising the Living God, the soldiers arrived shooting their guns. Bullets were passing right over our heads, but no one was killed. They arrested us and took us to the police station. I told them exactly what we had been doing.

That night as they held us there, we were happy. We felt strength. We began to praise God right at the police compound. In the morning, an official said, "You fools, the born-again! Go your way! Leave the police station."

So, about twenty of us left the police station praising and glorifying God!

~*~*~

SOLDIERS SEE ANGELS

Idi Amin also invaded the Kagela region in Tanzania and killed many people there. He claimed that the Kagela region was part of Uganda and that he was bringing back land which the Tanzanians had stolen from us. However, the Tanzanians fought and drove Idi Amin's army back to Uganda. The Tanzanians also came to our rescue by training Ugandans to fight Idi Amin. Thus, the war began which was intended to overthrow Idi Amin. The

29

Tanzanians knew that the only way to have peace was to work towards overthrowing Idi Amin.

So, the Tanzanian army along with the Ugandans who were trained in Tanzania joined hands and that war started in 1978. This was the war that brought down Idi Amin's government. The Libyans tried to help Idi Amin, but our God was faithful. As the war went on, the Tanzanians were gaining more and more ground, and the Libyans were loosing ground. Finally, in January of 1979, the Tanzanian army and the Ugandan rebels reached Kampala. They had fought their way from the Tanzania/Uganda border.

When Idi Amin was overthrown, many of his soldiers were running away because now the rebels were advancing towards the town to capture the town. Some of these soldiers which were fleeing met me and said, "Please, we know you. We know what you have been doing here. And we know that you have a Living God. Many times they sent us to kill you. However, every time we tried to do that, there was a voice which said, 'Don't do it!'

One time as we came we had determined to shoot all of you right on the spot as you were in the church praying. But, when we reached the church, we saw that angels had surrounded it. We knew they were angels because they were tall, tall men and there was a very powerful brightness. They had surrounded you. We were so amazed that we ran away for our lives. We know that the Living God is with you people."

Therefore, they asked me, "Will you please pray for us, that God may spare our lives?" So, I opened my Bible and witnessed to them. I shared with them the love that Jesus Christ has for them that forgives sin no matter how big the sin is. They confessed the salvation prayer. I prayed a prayer of faith with them. They were born-again. Those people are born-again even today.

~*~*~

JEWS HELD HOSTAGE

When the Palestinians hijacked France's airliner it was carrying many people including a great number of Jews. Many countries refused to allow this airliner to land in their country, but Idi Amin gave the Palestinians permission to land at Entebbe airport here in Uganda, our only international airport.

The Palestinians, along with Idi Amin, agreed to allow nationals from other countries to come off of the airliner and go their way. However, the Jews, which numbered about ninety (maybe more, I am no longer very sure) were refused permission to leave. Instead, Idi Amin agreed with the Palestinians to transport all the Jews from the plane to the old airport, which is in that same area.

The hijackers insisted that they were the only ones to guard the Jews inside and outside of that building until their demand was met by Israel. They went on to say that if their demand was not met, they were going to kill all of their Jewish hostages. We, as the underground church, which was known as Kabowa Redeemed Church of Christ, prayed for our Jewish brothers and sisters that the Lord may set them free. We immediately entered into a three day prayer and fasting for them.

Before Idi Amin had come into power there were many Jews in Uganda doing all kinds of work, one of those being construction. The Jews built a number of big buildings. Consequently, the Jews were the ones who had built the old airport, and had also started the building of the new airport. They knew both of those airports very well. So, at the same time that the Israelis were talking to the hijackers and Idi Amin, they were also planning an attack for the rescue of their people.

Soldiers were guarding the airport as the hijackers continued making all kinds of threats. One of the hostages, an elderly lady, fell very sick and was taken to Mulago Hospital, which is our largest hospital in Uganda. She was kept under heavy guard.

The day came, and I remember it well, when we as a church were praying in the "over-night". A good group of Christians were praying and fasting for the Jewish hostages. During that time of prayer, the Lord gave a vision to one of our sisters. She saw all the hostages at the airport freed and they were boarding a plane to go. She then heard a voice say, "The setting free of My people has come, but pray for your Brother Sempa, as he is at the airport."

It was at that very hour that night that the Israeli air force invaded the airport and killed Idi Amin's soldiers and the hijackers. They rescued all of the hostages, losing only one of their commandos.

When the Israelis had rescued the hostages, Idi Amin was so ashamed that he killed the lady hostage who had been taken to Mulago for treatment. And to this day, no one knows where her body was thrown.

A few months later, we got news from our brother Sempa who was one of Idi Amin's soldiers. He was praising the Lord as he gave us the testimony that he was the only one of all of Idi Amin's soldiers who had survived. Though his leg was injured, and later it was amputated, he was very thankful. He had survived.

We thanked God for the deliverance of our Jewish brothers and sisters, and also for our brother Sempa. (Sempa was very helpful in those days as he informed us in secret about Idi Amin's men and what they were planning to do to the church.) The time came after Idi Amin's overthrow, that Sempa left the army and came and joined the ministry. He started his own ministry in the western part of Uganda and the last time I heard from him fifteen years ago, he was doing a good work.

~*~*~

MIRACLE PROTECTION FOR PROSY

Prosy, a young sister from our church, was passing by the Lubiri army barracks on her way home. These barracks housed thousands of soldiers during the time of Idi Amin. The road Prosy was on was a well-traveled road.

Soldiers that were guarding the gate pulled Prosy off the road into the barracks and took her to a small room. On the floor of the room was much blood. There were knives and clubs lying around which had been used to kill people there.

More soldiers came to the room and it appeared that this room was used to rape women. One soldier commanded Prosy to undress herself, to take off all her clothes, so she did. The door was wide open and this soldier was going to rape this young girl right in the open in front of his fellow soldiers.

He advanced towards her as he was undressing himself. But, as he was doing that a very big heavenly star came out of nowhere through the door and stood between Prosy and him. That soldier ran away, as did all the other soldiers who were waiting their turn to rape her. They all just ran away.

Prosy was left there trembling. She had been praying in her heart, "Lord, save my life. Lord, spare my life. Lord, help me that these big evil men may not rape me. Lord, you have protected us many, many times." These were the words she told us she had prayed.

As Prosy stood there scared and trembling not knowing what to do, a soldier came in and told her to get dressed. He then escorted her to the gate. She came to us and gave that powerful testimony. We saw how God can take care of His people. We praised and thanked the Almighty God.

~*~*~

Questions & Answers

Q: Pastor Kaweesa, how did you plant churches during that difficult time?

A: During that time of the 70's, we did Surprise Open-Air meetings. In addition, a number of Christians opened their homes in different locations, so we had about seven different places that were "underground" churches. Christians gathered at these places at different days of the week. Sunday, one place, Monday, a different place and so on. So every day there was somewhere that was open for us to gather and pray.

We continually went and encouraged and strengthened the believers in Jesus' name. These places were around Kampala. Always we were on the move. We did not have bicycles. We did not have cars. We had nothing. We walked.

During this time of Idi Amin, we planted a number of churches that are still standing today. They are known as the Redeemed Churches of Christ. Many miracles took place in those meetings. God protected His people. We saw the mighty hand of the Almighty God.

Q: How were believers able to access Bibles? And, how did you train people?

A: When Idi Amin closed the churches, he left the Anglican Church, which is also called the Church of Uganda. The Church of Uganda uses the very same Bible we use. That church brought in Bibles and sold them to people through their bookstores.

Also, there were "good Samaritans" from the USA who tried to help us with reading materials. A number of times, Morris Cerrulo sent us materials concerning healing, deliverance, miracles, wonders, and how to evangelize. So, we got those kinds of books which really helped us a lot.

There was also an organization called the "New Wine" which smuggled materials into us. This encouraged us a lot. Also, in Kenya, there were meetings that we attended, although it was oftentimes very difficult for us to travel there from Uganda.

Anyone who got born-again during that time knew they would be killed. They read their Bibles constantly, memorized scriptures, and opened up their homes every night to be "praying houses".

We encouraged every Christian to, "Please, every night gather your people in your house, open your Bible, and read. Then, let each one in the house share something that the Lord is helping you to understand from that scripture." This built the Christians up in the Word of the Lord.

And with great power the apostles gave
witness to the resurrection of
the Lord Jesus Christ.
And great grace was upon them all.
Acts 4:33

~ Four ~

SETTING THE CAPTIVES FREE

The Spirit of the Lord is upon me,
because He has anointed me
to preach the gospel to the poor;
He has sent me to heal the brokenhearted,
to proclaim liberty to the captives
and recovery of sight to the blind,
to set at liberty those who are oppressed;
to proclaim the acceptable year of the Lord.
Luke 4:18,19

GIRL HEALED FROM COMA

When I had just become a "born-again", in my church I saw healings and demons cast out. One day I walked about six miles out to the village where my parents live. Muslim neighbors, who lived two houses from our home, had a dying daughter. She was in a coma.

It is the custom in our country to visit our neighbors when they have someone sick in the home. It is a time to offer them encouragement. So, I went to visit this family. Their living room was full of people. I announced to them, "I got born-again and I love God." I explained to them how I had seen the "born-agains" pray for people and how people were healed.

I went home, grabbed my Bible, and came back to the house where the girl lay dying. I did not know the right scripture, so I asked the Lord to give me the right scripture. The Lord helped me and I opened to a scripture in Matthew which said,

And Jesus went about all Galilee,
teaching in their synagogues,
preaching the gospel of the kingdom,
and healing all kinds of sickness
and all kinds of disease among the people.
Matthew 4:23

After reading the scripture, I told the people that this girl was going to be healed and I prayed in Jesus' name. After I had no more words to say, I announced, "She is healed." However, she did not appear to be healed.

I ran home and cried out to God, "Why wasn't she healed?" But, while I was praying, someone arrived at my door and questioned me, "What kind of God do you serve? Right as you left the girl rose up and was healed. They are even now preparing some tea for her."

I was very excited! I went back to the home. All the people were asking me questions. I didn't know very much in the Bible yet, so I was simply telling them, "Jesus heals. Jesus heals. Jesus loves you. Jesus loves you."

From that time, I felt that I could serve God. When I went back to the city to go to school, I went to the hospitals and visited the sick people, very, very sick people. I would lay my hands on them and tell them that Jesus heals. God performed miracle after miracle.

~*~*~

THROAT CANCER HEALED

One day I visited a woman in the hospital who was suffering from throat cancer. Cancer had eaten the whole throat, so she was fed through tubes. I ministered to this lady and told her that we were going to believe God for her deliverance. She had been in the hospital for one year.

After we prayed, I gave her a glass of water and told her to drink it. She listened and did it. She was checked by the doctors and they could not find the cancer anymore. Three days later we received news that she was totally and completely healed. She left the hospital.

~*~*~

UNEXPLAINED BLEEDING STOPS

Another time, there was a dying child in the hospital. She was bleeding and the doctors did not know why. The mother was crying and wailing. I told the mother about the love of Jesus and that the child would be healed.

We laid our hands on the child and the bleeding stopped. The child was totally and completely healed.

~*~*~

MYSTERIOUS EYE SICKNESS HEALED

On another trip to the hospital, we found a lady who had a terrible eye sickness. The doctors did not know what kind of eye sickness it was. She had suffered with it for over ten years and had gone to many doctors. She had even visited the witch doctors before finally going to the hospital.

As I ministered to her, she became born-again. I told her, "Jesus is alive, and He is going to heal you." As I laid hands on her, she was completely healed. She was discharged from the hospital.

~*~*~

LADY DELIVERED FROM GOITERS

One lady was suffering from a goiter. You know goiters, they are so big and they are right in front of your throat. Some grow very big. This goiter was quite large.

The lady said, "I want to be healed of this goiter. It bothers me a lot." I laid my hand upon her and prayed and prayed.

I told her, "I believe that the Lord is going to operate on you." After my prayer, nothing seemed to be changing, and she went back home.

But, in one week's time that goiter had completely disappeared! It was no longer there. She was totally healed! She came to church and gave her testimony and we praised the Almighty God!

"We minister in hospitals as well as on the streets. Many are encouraged and we are encouraged. Friend, I want to tell you, the healing ministry is present today. I have seen many miracles. Even in this time of freedom, we have seen healings. They bring us sick people to pray for." - Pastor Kaweesa

~*~*~

PARALYZED WOMAN SET FREE

Back in the 1970's, a woman came and asked me to go to a certain village to pray for her parents. Her parents were not born-again. We made arrangements, and I along with three sisters from the church traveled to her parent's home.

As we arrived, we found that many of the neighbors were also there at her parent's home. As is the custom in our country, we were greeted. Oftentimes, the greetings can go on for quite a long time, especially when we are greeting someone that we have not seen for a long time.

As one neighbor lady was greeting me, the Lord took me in a vision to her house. I saw her yard in which there was a very big tree. It was the type of tree used by witchdoctors to make herbs. They also use this type of tree to consult certain spirits. *(Herbs are a type of witchcraft, or "medicine", made from roots, parts of bat wings, and other traditionally "spiritual" items.)*

In this vision, the Lord led me inside her house and I saw the color of the mat in the corner. I moved ahead to the bedroom of this lady while in this vision. I saw her bed, which had a blanket running all the way to the floor. Kneeling down, I looked under the bed where I saw an African basket that was full of witchcraft. I heard the Lord's voice say, "Tell her to go bring that basket of witchcraft, and then you shall pray for her."

So, after she had greeted me, I told her, "I have been to your house." I began describing the house. Then, I

43

asked her, "Do you know your bedroom very well?" She answered, "Yes."

I said, "Under your bed, there is a basket of witchcraft. Go and bring it back here and I will pray for you. You need to receive Jesus Christ as your personal Savior and Lord."

Without hesitation, she ran away trembling. She ran through the village shouting, "Come and see these born-again people! Come and see! They have told me everything which I did!" She was like the Samaritan woman who went to the village telling everyone to come and see the prophet (Jesus) who told her everything she ever did.

About an hour later, I saw her coming back carrying the big basket on her head. Behind her, were over one hundred people following. When I saw what was happening, I was a bit afraid and I asked, "Lord, what is this? What have you done? Don't you know they have refused us to preach the gospel? Remember our churches have been closed. I just came here to pray for this house. What am I going to do with all of these people?"

Then I heard a voice say, "Go out and minister to those people." So, I did.

I told the sisters who had come with me to begin singing. They began singing songs of praise. I then told them to give testimonies. The sisters gave their testimonies of how they had come to know the Lord Jesus Christ. After they had done that I started preaching and as I preached all fear left me.

People got born-again. We broke the power of witchcraft and prayed for those people. As we prayed for them healings took place. What is amazing is that God baptized some of them with the Holy Spirit! There was jubilation right there in that service!

A lady was possessed with a demon and the devil in her started screaming and crying and begging. I cast it out in Jesus' name. After we had done all that, we burned the witchcraft in the basket. Even other people brought in their witchcraft and we burned it.

Then, a lady came and said, "We have a very sick person. She is completely paralyzed. She is lame in both arms and legs, she cannot do anything at all. Can you please come and pray for her?"

I had not really gotten the picture of the person she was talking about. And because I was very excited about seeing what God had just done, I answered her, "Oh, yes, yes! We shall come!"

This lady led us, along with the whole group we were with. Even people along the way, once they saw us headed to that poor woman's house, joined us. We came to a small hut. There she was, completely twisted, completely paralyzed. I asked her how long she had been that way. She said for over thirty years. She could not move. She could do nothing. There was a young man taking her to and from her hut.

Inside, I was struggling. I prayed in my heart, "Lord, what now? How can I help this kind of person?" The Lord encouraged me. He gave me His Word. He is the Lord who made the blind to see, who made the lame to walk, and brought the dead back to life.

I said, "Lord, You are able." I shared with her about the love of Jesus Christ. She accepted Christ. As I was going to pray, I said to all the people, "Please, don't close your eyes." Our custom, normally, is to close our eyes when we pray. But, sometimes the Lord may tell you to not close your eyes. That is what the Lord told me to tell those people.

I told them, "We are born-again. We only preach the Word of the Lord. The Lord whom we serve is alive! It is the Lord who is going to heal this lady, not witchcraft, not witchdoctors or Muhammad. It is Jesus Christ, the Son of the Living God! He is able to perform a miracle in this woman's life!" So, everyone stayed watching.

We prayed and prayed and rebuked those evil spirits of lameness. We broke those evil spirits in the name of Jesus. After a long time of prayer, we were done and nothing had happened. So, I encouraged this lady that the Lord had healed her. We left and went home to our village.

After three days we received this report. As the paralyzed woman was on her bed Jesus came to her in a vision. She saw Him very clearly. Jesus took hold of her right arm and said to her, "From the time they prayed for you, I healed you. Rise up! Go and preach the Gospel from this day forth!" When Jesus left, she found herself standing by the bed. Her legs were normal, her arms were normal. She was completely and totally healed instantly! She was very happy.

In the morning, she ran through the whole village shouting, "You know me! You know me! You know me! They prayed for me. I was lame. I couldn't do anything. I was very sick, but the Lord healed me!"

That lady was totally and completely healed. She married and is even now preaching the gospel.

~*~*~

"Oh my, God is so powerful. God is so wonderful. God performs miracles!

My Friend, when God speaks, please obey what He has spoken. It may be only one or two words. However, the miracle that the Lord will perform out of that will be beyond your imagination." - Pastor Kaweesa

LADY HEALED OF CANCER

A lady came to our church who had suffered with cancer for quite a long time. After I had preached, I invited those who wanted to get born-again, because that is what we do first. After that, I called for those who were sick. I began naming the sicknesses and prayed.

However, this lady later told us as she gave her testimony that she did not come forward because I did not name her sickness. She was suffering from cancer. As we were praying for sick people, she prayed, "Lord, even though they have not mentioned my sickness, Lord, You know my sickness. I know that You can heal me. Heal me, Lord."

Therefore, it happened that while she was praying, she received a vision from the Lord. She saw a white sheet come down. On every corner of the sheet, there was a hand touching it. On the sheet, she saw all kinds of medical instruments used for operations. Hands took the

47

instruments and started operating on her tummy. The hands took out a certain tumor, which she explained, "...looked very, very funny".

After the hands had taken out the tumor, they put back everything in order in the tummy. She then heard a voice say, "Today you have been healed of cancer." When she came out of that vision, she was very excited. She said, "Lord, You have healed me of cancer!"

After three days, she went to her doctor. She felt well. She did not feel any kind of weakness. She knew that Jesus had healed her. When she went to her doctor, he checked her. And they checked and checked and checked. She was totally and completely delivered.

"Miracles of healing are still happening. I have always served the Lord under the anointing of miracles and wonders. I have not backed down on that. The Lord has been so faithful right here where I am serving. He is faithful in every step I take. In all the places I go, I see miracles and wonders. God is a miracle working God!" - Pastor Kaweesa

~*~*~

Question & Answer

Q: Pastor Kaweesa, what did you do after you finished school?

A: I began to pastor in my first year of High School. I went to school until midday and then every night I spent praying in one of our prayer places. Each night we were

somewhere praying. My aunt was very happy with me, seeing the zeal of God in me. I was growing in the Lord to become a mighty man of God.

There were no Bible colleges in Uganda during the time of Idi Amin. I completed a correspondence course from a Bible college in Nairobi and received a diploma for that. It was not easy going to High School, ministering every night and also doing all the work of the correspondence courses, but by God's grace I did it. The course was free because they knew that Uganda was closed to the Gospel. The only expense that I could meet was to mail the material back after I had done the work they had given me.

After I finished High School, I went into full-time ministry. I was already doing almost full-time ministry. We continued to evangelize. Many people were coming to the Lord, even soldiers.

One soldier came in plain clothes, bringing his son whom was paralyzed. At first, he did not introduce himself as a soldier. We prayed for his son and God performed a miracle instantly. That young man was completely and totally healed! He threw away his crutches. We told him to run around and he did run around.

So, these two men were so happy. They announced to us, "Before today we were soldiers, we were officials in Idi Amin's army. But from today on, we are born-again." Those soldiers got born-again! They started attending our church. The Lord is so amazing. Every time these soldiers came to church, they brought us secrets concerning the churches and what Idi Amin planned to do. So, that helped us a lot.

When a man's ways please the Lord,
He makes even his enemies to
Be at peace with him.
Proverbs 16:7

~ *Five* ~

NOT ALONE

*Yes, my brother, let me have
joy from you in the Lord;
Refresh my heart in the Lord.*
Philemon 20

Steven Kaweesa

PERSECUTED, BUT NOT FORSAKEN

During the time of Idi Amin's rule there were no missionaries who dared to come to Uganda. When Idi Amin threw out the Indians, he also threw out the whites and all missionaries. The door was closed.

During that time, we traveled to Kenya to attend Bible conferences even though it was very difficult. From Kampala to the border of Kenya there were over twelve roadblocks that we had to pass through. At these roadblocks we had to take out our luggage. Each piece was then opened and searched for guns and money. We hid our money right down under our underpants. That was the way our money could survive.

One time, we were traveling to a conference in Nairobi where we planned to stay for two months. After about six or seven roadblocks, we came to a certain roadblock. We were kind of foolish, but I'm glad we were foolish for the Lord, for in our luggage, we had our Bibles.

We opened our bags in which we had stored the Bibles. The guard saw our Bibles and pulled us out and put us in a line. When someone was taken out and put aside, they knew that their time may be coming to an end very soon. Thousands who were "put aside" lost their lives in front of a firing squad. Five of us were put aside.

The soldier charged us, "What is the meaning of this Bible? Who are you? Where are you going? What are you going to do? Why are you leaving this country? Who has invited you?"

I answered, "I am a servant of God. I am a Born-again. I am going to Nairobi." I didn't tell him where I was going to visit. Inside each one of our hearts we were praying and calling upon the name of the Lord. We prayed, "Lord, we are going to learn more from Your Word. Lord, don't give us into the hands of these evil men." So we were praying and praying.

We thought that we were going to be taken somewhere. A number of times we had seen people seized and taken somewhere, and that was the end. The soldiers accused you of being a rebel against the government and that you wanted to overthrow the government. You were a "bad guy". So they had to put you in the prison and they had to torture you with all those methods which I told you about before. They were able to justify anything.

Eventually, we were told, "You stupid fellows! You fools! Do you think that we don't know what you are doing? Okay, you go!" We thanked God as we got back on the bus. This was our seventh army roadblock, and we still had another five ahead of us, but the Lord was so good. We went through all of the remaining roadblocks and entered Kenya. We then went on to Nairobi and to our seminar.

Kenya is where most of the Bible seminars took place. It was not easy for a minister from Uganda to go, but I thank God that He gave us the strength to go each time that we had the opportunity to go there.

~*~*~

$30 PER MONTH AND A BICYCLE

Some missionaries helped us. One organization was called the "Open Doors". They wanted to help ministers in persecuted countries, so this included Uganda. They met us in Kenya and offered us assistance. Like for me, they offered thirty dollars per month. That sounds like very little, but I tell you that it was a very big encouragement to me and my family.

So, they gave me thirty dollars every month and they also gave me a bicycle. I was able to get that bicycle into Uganda because Uganda had no problem with bicycles. I used that bicycle to evangelize, to reach out to people.

It was a great relief to get the bicycle, since we had to walk on our feet everywhere we went. We had no money for a taxi, and no other means of transportation, not even a bicycle. I started reaching out to places that I could not reach on foot.

But, it happened one night as we were in night prayer at our church that soldiers came in and grabbed us. They tortured us and beat some of our friends all during that night. Then, they left us alone, but they went away with my new bicycle. They took two bicycles from us that night, one from another brother.

So, I lost my bicycle. I felt so bad. But, on the other hand, I felt good. I said, "Lord, I thank you for the time I have used that bicycle. And, I thank you, Lord, that you have more bicycles than that one. I thank you that you have more bicycles in your store." So, I was a bit happy on the other side. And also, I was happy that they did not kill us that night. The Lord had placed His protection around us.

~*~*~

GOD'S HAND EXTENDED

My wife and I were married in a very difficult time. Neither of us had a job, except that I was a pastor to the "underground" church. Our church members were unable to give much support. Many could not find jobs.

The monthly salary I was getting was enough to live for seven days. Then, the rest of the month we had to live by faith and from the "sympathizers". It was a very difficult situation. Day by day, it was a great hardship to take care of my family. Time and time again, we had no food. I had nowhere to go, nowhere to turn. We had spent my little salary.

In the beginning we didn't know much about children. I didn't know that my wife was not giving enough milk for our first daughter who was becoming thin and crying continually. A lady at the church realized what was wrong and rushed to get milk for the baby. The baby drank the milk, was satisfied and slept. We then feared that our baby would eventually die from hunger. Crying, we knelt down, and asked God to help us. From then on, that woman gave us a bottle of milk everyday.

There were many times when there was not enough food. Like one time, we did not have food at all and had not eaten for two days. We were praying and calling on the name of the Lord. There was no money in the church. We did not feel right to go and beg, so we prayed.

A brother heard God tell him, "Go and bring Pastor Steve some food." So, he brought us all kinds of food.

This type of provision came to us a number of times. Now we have needs, but it is not as severe as when we were dying from hunger in those days.

~*~*~

NO FOOD IN THE HOUSE . . . AGAIN

On one particular Saturday we had no food. We were wondering what we would do on Sunday. We had to walk about five miles to go to church in the morning and then walk back to our home. That is what we did for several years. We did not mind doing that. We were always happy to walk those miles for God.

That Saturday at about four o'clock, miraculously, a brother came and brought a lot of food to us, as well as money. He explained to us that he was on his way home when he heard a voice tell him, "Take food to Pastor Kaweesa." So, he went to the market and bought food. And, he even brought cash!

We were very, very, very thankful. God fed us that day. The money he gave me was enough to take us through the whole month. God gave us food for the whole month!

~*~*~

THREE THOUSAND SHILLINGS!

There was another time when we again had no food. We had two children at that time and nowhere to turn for help. The day went by and I had looked for money everywhere. Our friends had no money or food. By seven o'clock, my wife and I knew that we were going to spend the whole night hungry. Weeping, I prayed, "Lord, we would have stayed the whole night without food, but these little children...." I did not want even my wife to see I was crying.

As I prayed, deep inside, I was a bit assured that food was coming. I wondered from where as it was almost time to go to bed. Before long, a brother arrived at our house. He had come all the way from a different area, about fifty miles away.

This brother said, "Steve, I am not going to stay, but I just wanted to pass by and find out how you are doing. Are you doing fine? Are you okay?" At that time, I needed about a hundred Ugandan shillings. We needed a hundred shillings just to survive.

This brother was going to his Auntie's house, and as he was leaving he asked, "Do you want some money?" He actually asked me that question. If they asked you that question, what would you answer? You can guess! Let me tell you what I said.

I answered him, "Yes, I want some money."

He then asked me, "How much?"

I replied, "Well, I don't know how much you have, but you can give me as the Lord leads you." What I had answered was very, very right. Why? Because this guy had a lot of money!

He pulled out a bundle of ten thousand shillings, which was a lot of money back in those days. It was a bundle. He began counting it out. He counted one hundred, two hundred, and three hundred. He passed through one thousand, two thousand, and he counted to three thousand shillings! Uganda shillings! He pulled out three thousand. My eyes were so wide open! In my heart, I was so happy. I was wondering, "Is it really true? Is it really going to happen?" He then handed me those three thousand shillings!

I was so happy! I accompanied him out the door, then went back into the house and danced and jumped and shouted! After that, I went and bought everything which we needed. The Lord had provided for us once again.

~*~*~

MIRACLE OF ONE SHOE

It so happened that I had only one shoe. I didn't have other shoes at that time and I didn't have enough money to buy another shoe. I was walking to minister at the church, which was five miles away.

One day on a Wednesday the rain poured very heavily. My old shoe had holes all over in the bottom of it. As I walked to church on those muddy roads of Africa, my shoe soaked up with mud and water.

The church we had at that time did not have money for chairs. The people had to sit on the floor. We put mats on the floor for people to sit on. So, you would have to take off your shoes so you would not make the mats muddy. Then, when your friend comes to sit, he may sit comfortably. Even me, a preacher, I had to take off my shoe.

Now you can imagine, a pastor who is going to preach, and mud had soaked into my sock. It was very, very

59

dirty. That day I felt so bad, I said, "No, Lord, this has to stop. A minister cannot continue like this. With all the shoes in this country, You have some shoes for me."

"My Friend, don't take things for granted. You may think that shoes and clothes are not very important. But, I tell you, that someone in a certain country, someone in the world today, needs that shoe, and needs those clothes. It is very important to him or to her. And so, that's the way it was for me. I was praying for just a shoe." - Pastor Kaweesa

So, I took off my shoe, took off my sock, washed my feet and went to the pulpit barefooted and preached the Word of the Lord. The Spirit of God came down and ministered to the people. People were delivered of demonic possession. It was quite wonderful and I didn't even care that I was barefooted, because I was so much encouraged at what the Lord was doing. I knew that God was training me in His own way.

However, I determined that my situation had to stop. So, I sent the message that I was not going to go home today. I was going to fast and pray and seek the face of the Lord for at least three days. What was I praying for? What was I going to fast for? I was going to pray and fast for a shoe. I wanted shoes for my feet! I am a minister. I have to dress in a decent manner, in a manner which gives glory to the Almighty God.

So, I started praying. The first day went by. The second day went by. The third day came. On the evening of the third day, a brother came to me right where I was. I opened the door for him. When he came in, he said, "Steve, I came from Nairobi two days ago where I had bought this shoe and some clothes. When I was asleep, I heard a voice tell me to take that shoe which I had bought and give it to you. The Lord told me that you were praying."

When this brother awoke, he was very happy and excited! He said, "Thank you, God! I believe that. Let me even put in some pants and shirts and I'm also going to give him some money!" So, he came and told me, "Steve, I have brought you this. This is what the Lord told me to do."

When I got that, I was so excited. I was very thankful to God. I said, "Lord, God, thank You very, very much. You are my provider."

From that time, I have never lacked shoes on my feet. I broke that curse. It really was a curse. I broke it in the name of Jesus Christ. The Lord is so good. God can clothe His people. Amen.

"My Friend, God gave His best. We, as Christians, if we say that we love God and that we love our fellow man, then it is our obligation and duty to give. The Lord has taught me that I should be a giver.

Giving makes you happy. When you give to someone, you feel so nice. You feel uplifted. I encourage Christians that it is our responsibility to give where it is necessary, and to give with an open heart. The Lord is faithful. The Lord is going to bless you." – Kaweesa

~*~*~

Question & Answer

Q: Pastor Kaweesa, after all that you have gone through, what would you say is the key to living a life that is fully blessed by God? And, how can people raise their faith to believe God in a situation that looks like there is no way, where there is no provision and it looks like nothing is coming?

A: First, you have to trust God. You must have faith in the Lord. You have to know that the One you have believed in is alive. Then, pray. Call upon His name. If you lack anything, pray. And, when you pray, trust and believe that the good Lord is going to provide.

Another thing, do your work diligently. Do what you are told faithfully. Because, what you do to others, that is what will return to you. If you are a servant of God, serve faithfully. Whether an usher, or an evangelist, or pastor. Whatever the Lord has called you to do, serve your church faithfully. In return, expect to be given back abundantly. You may not know where God is going to give you the return, but expect from the Lord. As I have done that, the Lord has been so faithful. He has met my needs. I have even been given land.

As a pastor, I do not only preach in the pulpit on Sundays. During the week, I find time to go and visit the people, born-again people, as well as, not born-again people. Even in the born-again people's homes, there are often those that are not born-again, so I go to them.

One day when I was out visiting, I came to a home where there was an elderly man who was not born-again. I shared with him how Jesus Christ had come to save, and how Jesus loves him.

This old man said, "Okay, I have heard all that, my son." Then, he asked me a question, "But, my son....." He called me 'my son'.

I replied, "Yes, Sir?"

He asked me, "Have you built a house?"

I answered, "No, I have never built a house." At that time I had no house of my own.

He explained, "I have land to offer to you. Tomorrow, come here and I will show you the land."

So, I went there the next day, and that man gave me one and a half acres of land! That was a great blessing to me! But, how did I get that? I was right on the job. The Lord found me on the job. And, the Lord will find you right where you are. The Lord has supplied many of my needs right on my job. People have desired to do things for me or to give to me because they love me and because they saw the need. I don't tell them my need, but they do what they do by themselves because God touches them.

So, do the right thing. Serve God faithfully. Do what you are supposed to do. Do not be discouraged. Sometimes it seems you will never have the things you pray and trust God for, however, in due time you will get whatever God has designed for you to have.

Do not be deceived,
God is not mocked;
for whatever a man sows,
that he will also reap.
For he who sows to his flesh
will of the flesh reap corruption,
but he who sows to the Spirit
will of the Spirit reap everlasting life.
And let us not grow weary while doing good,
for in due season we shall reap
if we do not lose heart.
Therefore, as we have opportunity,
let us do good to all,
especially to the household of faith.
Galatians 6:7-10

~ Six ~

WINDS OF WAR RAGE ON

God is our refuge and strength,
a very present help in trouble.
Therefore, we will not fear,
even though the earth be removed,
and though the mountains be carried
into the midst of the sea....
The Lord of hosts is with us;
The God of Jacob is our refuge
Psalm 46: 1, 2, 7

BULLETS LIKE RAINDROPS

The fighting between the rebels and Idi Amin's soldiers continued as the rebels attempted to overthrow Idi Amin. We were on the run because soldiers had overtaken our area. We were running aimlessly, not knowing where to go.

One particular time, as the fighting broke out, I was in town. Not knowing what was happening to my wife and children back at home, I began running on the road trying to get to them. It was nearly ten miles back to my home.

As others and I were running, the fighting broke out around us. The exchange of gunfire was very, very heavy forcing us at times to take cover and lie down on the ground. Bullets fell aimlessly like raindrops upon us. Hundreds of people were hit by the falling bullets. But, God is so good. Although I saw the bullets falling right beside me, ahead of me, and at my feet, the Lord protected me. No single bullet hit me.

You shall not be afraid of the terror by night,
nor of the arrow that flies by day....
A thousand may fall at your side,
and ten thousand at your right hand;
But it shall not come near you.
Psalm 91: 5, 7

As the guns became silent, I looked around and saw that many had died. Those of us who had survived rose up. I looked at myself. I had no wounds at all! We began running once again. We ran and ran and ran. And, as we did, the gunfire started again.

A bullet passed right over my head. I heard it pass right over my hair. There was a lady who was running in front of me. A bullet hit her, going deep inside her head and she fell down. There was nothing we could do to help her. We just continued to run.

God helped us and we came out of that fire exchange. The Lord had spared my life that day. Had He not, I would have been dead by now. Finally, I made it home to my family and found that they were safe. We went far away. The Lord protects His people.

~*~*~

SAFETY ON THE FRONTLINES

At three o'clock one morning we awoke to gunshots. The rebels had advanced towards our home area. Idi Amin's soldiers had arrived and we began to hear heavy gunfire right around us. There was a large amount of firepower, big guns and small guns. Although it was night, we saw light from their weapons. We heard houses falling down from the bombs.

As daybreak came we saw the soldiers and their thousands. We could also see on the other side the rebels and their thousands. We had nowhere to go. The fighting continued.

I was in a very small house with my wife, who was pregnant with our first child, and we were taking care of two other children at that time. When the guns became quiet, we would try to come out as did other families, but we were unable to. We were right on the frontlines.

The guns continued throughout the whole day. After the fighting, I saw that many soldiers had died, many rebels had died, and many civilians had died. There was death everywhere. Houses had been hit. It was a very terrifying time. We could not stomach it to look on the dead bodies and all the blood that was flowing in our home area.

But, once again, God had been merciful to us. My family was safe. God had spared us that day and we gave thanks to the Almighty God. The fighting continued for many days, and we could not leave our home.

~*~*~

"ADVANCE! SHOOT!"

During that time of war, many people lost their lives. It was terrible. We were forced to run from our home area. My wife, myself and our children, along with some of the other villagers fled about ten miles. We came to an area that had been captured by the rebels. Government forces had not been able to reach that area. The rebels were now the "good guys". They were fighting for the cause of rescuing us from the tyranny of the murderous rule of Idi Amin.

In this area, we found a lady who had a house with several rooms she was renting out. We got two rooms, one for the ladies and children, and one for several men including myself. While we were there, the soldiers invaded the area. We were in the hands of the rebels, and the soldiers were advancing. There was very, very heavy fighting. The small house we were in was shaking and shaking. My wife and some of the other ladies could not stomach it and ran outside. They were very scared and confused. The safest thing to do was to stay right where we were, but the ladies went out because they thought that the house was going to fall on them.

We heard the captains of the rebels shout over the firing, "Advance! Advance! Go ahead! Shoot!" Those were the words which we heard and it was very, very frightening. We were praying and praying. We could not pray out loud, we were praying right in our spirits. Each one prayed, "Oh, Lord, clean my heart. If it is my time to die, let me die in Your hands." Eventually, the rebels managed to push the armies of the government miles back. Hundreds had died. Many rebels lost their lives.

When we discovered that our ladies were gone, we feared that they had died. We looked for their bodies among those of the dead soldiers. When we could not find them there, we feared that they had been taken. In time, however, the ladies came out from where they had been hiding. We praised and thanked God that he spared the ladies and our children.

That was not the end of the fighting, but we went on.

"I want to let you know that God protects His people. In such circumstances where war breaks out, the hand of God is unto those that love the Lord. That is what happened to us. The hand of God was right upon us." - Pastor Kaweesa

~*~*~

A Vision from the Lord . . .

I saw myself in a very big church with several thousand people. There were blacks, whites, many different people. We were all praising God. There were many instruments. The choir was praising God. A voice told me, "What you have seen, you are about to see."

I said, "My God! Idi Amin is going soon! Lord, You are going to lift this country from its bondage, to bring revival to Uganda!" I shared with my brothers what I had seen and we were very encouraged. We knew that the time of Idi Amin was soon to come to an end.

I talk about these visions because they were very powerful.

A Brother's Vision . . .

He saw a very big mountain. It had an active volcano that was spewing fire. Lava was flowing in different directions. A voice told him, "The persecution is coming to an end in Uganda. And after that, revival is coming, not only to Uganda, but it will go to other nations of the world."

71

We were so encouraged! We knew that God was showing us that we were going to be a part of this new revival.

~*~*~

WINDS OF CHANGE BEGIN TO BLOW

In 1978, rebel soldiers came from Tanzania. The fighting went on for several months. Many unfortunate, innocent people died during this time of conflict. Many villages were utterly destroyed.

Idi Amin's soldiers were on one side, rebels were on the other. Bullets were flying over our heads. I didn't think we were going to make it. We didn't know how or where to take cover, but once again the good Lord spared our lives.

Idi Amin was overthrown in 1979, and because we had gone through so much, we were very happy. We thought that now the time of freedom had come. However, the fighting was not over yet.

The Lord brought to me another vision:

I saw a Roman soldier with an arrow. He shot and the arrow went up. I also saw a small river like the River Nile, not flowing with water, but with blood. A voice said, "The suffering is not yet ended. But after the suffering, the revival will come."

We were very disappointed. I told my fellow brothers that I could not believe this, and I told the Lord that I must leave the country. I said that I **must** leave. Morris Cerullo had previously invited us to come to the United States, but we were unable to go and we were very much disappointed.

~*~*~

NEW PRESIDENTS, NEW PROBLEMS

The fighting was not over. There were internal problems in the new government and the new president, Yusuf Lula, was overthrown in a matter of a few days. After that, came another man, Godfrey Binaisa. He was a good man, but there was division. Those left from Idi Amin began torturing and killing people. Within a few months, our hope was gone. Soldiers began killing people again just as they had in Idi Amin's time. They also started fighting among themselves, fighting for power. This led to more suffering and more people continued to die. I saw people dying.

During this time, the soldiers came to my house several times. They also came to the church. One time as I was at the church praying, the Spirit of God commanded me, "Leave this place now! If you don't, you are going to die!" Quickly, I left and went to my house.

The next day when I returned, an old man explained to me how after I had left the day before, ten soldiers came. The soldiers demanded of him, "Where is your young man?"

He had answered them, "I don't have any young man". The soldiers then killed fifteen people there in that village. It was very frightening. This kind of suffering continued on and lasted for a complete year.

Then, another ruler came on the scene, named Paul Muwanga. He promised that he was going to put elections in place. However, he already had someone to put in office. There was an election, and what was amazing, was that the man who didn't win the election was the one put into authority. It was the former one in power before Idi Amin came into power, Milton Obote. He brought more and more pain.

There was more fighting, shooting and killing during this entire time. You had to be very careful. The whole country was in total confusion. We continued to pray for our country. The war continued in an attempt to overthrow the president. Many villages were destroyed where everyone was killed, no one spared, not even a chicken. People fled for their lives. There was much suffering.

Roadblocks were put up everywhere. One time, at one particular roadblock, a soldier took me out and told me that I was a rebel. This is what they did to people, and then, they would kill them. I told the soldier, "I am a minister of the Gospel." He laughed and said that he had been a Christian at one time, but had forsaken the way of the Lord. He let me go. My life was spared.

~*~*~

"GOD, PROTECT US"

In the early 1980's, after Idi Amin was overthrown, soldiers came during the night and surrounded my house. Although Idi Amin had been overthrown, we were still experiencing very difficult situations. Soldiers were stealing and killing, as well as kidnapping people.

That particular night, soldiers were breaking into houses and taking all of the men that they could get a hold of. My brother, who was sleeping in the living room, looked out the window. He saw that the whole building, in which I was renting an apartment, was surrounded with soldiers. He ran to my room and shouted, "The soldiers have come! What are we going to do?"

I told him, "Get on your knees!" We went right down to our knees and began to pray. We prayed, "God, please help us. Cover us with your blood. Protect us from these murderers." The soldiers were there until six o'clock in the morning at which time they left. When we came out of the house we found women weeping and crying. Their husbands had been kidnapped and taken away. Much property had been stolen. Those men who were taken have never been seen again, even up until today.

Jesus protected us. Otherwise, we would not have survived.

~*~*~

ANGELS SURROUND US

Although Idi Amin had been overthrown, the fighting continued. We did not see much difference. The new government was kidnapping and killing people, also. Although people had the freedom to pray, soldiers went from house to house torturing people, born-agains and not born-agains. The soldiers invaded village after village. They would surround villages and shoot everyone. Houses were blown up. There was much suffering and pain. I don't know how many people died. The Lord spared our lives. It was a miracle, as we were right in the war zone. For over eight years this continued. Day after

75

day, we heard stories of people being killed here and there.

One time, as we were having an "over-night", about seven of us were praying and seeking the face of the Almighty God. Some of the soldiers tried to come in. What followed was this: I saw angels surround us. Angels surrounded the entire building so that the soldiers could not reach us. That is exactly what happened. The soldiers left and went on their way. We thanked the Lord, the Almighty God, for that wonderful protection. We were thankful that at such a time like that, God's angels were there to protect us. God has protected us in quite a number of ways.

~*~*~

SOLDIERS LOSE DESIRE TO KILL

On one of the Friday night "over-night" meetings, about seventy of us Christians had gathered to pray. We went ahead and prayed as we always do. About midnight, as I was preaching, I heard the voice of the Lord speak to me, "Stop preaching! Tell the Christians to start praying because the enemy is coming. My hand of protection is upon you."

I stopped preaching and told the Christians to start praying. Each one of us went down on our knees. We cried to the Lord for over an hour. When I opened my eyes, over twenty soldiers had surrounded us. We had no where to escape, but at that moment, deep in my heart, I felt confident that the Lord was with us.

As all of us were silent, the captain said to us, "We have the power to kill you." Then, he went on to say that they felt that they were not going to kill us, and that he didn't even know why they were there.

He said, "The only thing that we want from you is for you to help us by showing us our way back to our barracks." Two of our brothers gave themselves up and led the soldiers to their barracks, which were about two miles away. We prayed for our two brothers as they were gone. Then, after about an hour later, they came back. We rejoiced that night. The great God put His protection around us!

In the morning as we were going back to our homes, we got news that this very same group of soldiers had killed over ten men on the other side of the village. They had gone from house to house snatching men. They had then taken those men to the middle of the road and killed them. From there, the soldiers had come to our church. But, the good Lord did not allow them to do us harm.

God knows His people. In times of trouble when we call on Him, He hears us, and comes and saves us.

~*~*~

ROWDY THIEVES INVADE

We eat our dinner quite late here in Uganda. It is not like in the West. Oftentimes we eat at eight or nine o'clock, sometimes even as late as ten o'clock. Much of this is due to the children having to do their homework until quite late. The children must do their homework or they are punished quite severely in the schools here in Uganda. They have to spank these kids if they don't do

77

their homework. So, in a number of homes, they eat a bit late, us inclusive.

One evening at about nine o'clock, the Lord spoke to me very clearly and said, "Thieves are coming to steal from this village, but My blood has covered you."

So, I told my wife and children, "Please let us get together, and let us pray right now for our village. And let us bind that evil spirit of stealing and killing." As we were praying for the blood of Jesus to cover us and protect us, the murderers and thieves were on their way to our village.

As soon as we had finished praying, we heard shooting. The shooting was coming from all directions. I heard the huge sound of breaking glass and doors breaking. All of a sudden we heard screaming and crying, "They are killing us! They are killing us!" We were afraid, but as we continued praying, we felt the presence of God. After about two hours, the disturbance stopped.

In the morning, we discovered that the thieves had stolen food from about five houses. But, no one was killed and we were very thankful to God for that. Although much property was lost, no lives were lost.

~*~*~

LEOPARD FINDS OUR PRAYER PLACE

In 1981, seven of us men spent all night on a hill praying and calling on the name of the Living God. We were in a bushy, forested area, an area that we used many times to pray. No one knew that there was a leopard on this hill.

Although we have leopards here in Africa, they are mainly found in the National Parks. They cannot be found just everywhere. Some people that come from the West think that you can see leopards anywhere at any place. It is not like that.

We had made a fire and were praying and seeking the face of the Lord. We had read scriptures and discussed them. Each one had shared and given a testimony. We then stood up, moved around, and prayed for things that the Lord had placed on our hearts.

After praying, we would come back to the fire and share. If someone had been praying and the Lord had given him a vision, he would share that as well as any words of encouragement the Lord had given. If you needed to be prayed for, then, we would pray. And if you needed to praise, then, we would praise the Lord together. Right around three o'clock in the morning we came back to our fire.

It so happened that a leopard came right up near to us in the dark. Although there was a fire, we could not see very far. One of us thought that the shadow we were seeing was a dog, but when we looked closer, we saw that it was not a dog. There is no dog that is big like that in our country.

Instead of advancing toward us, the leopard turned around and started making a crying sound. We knew the voice of the leopards, how they make their noise. Once we were certain that it was a leopard we started praying, "Jesus, close the mouth of that leopard." In the name of Jesus, we prayed that it would just run away and go very, very far.

That is exactly what happened. That leopard went right on crying and crying until it disappeared into the forest. We praised and thanked God for that wonderful protection. The hand of God was upon us once again.

~*~*~

Questions & Answers

Q: Did you see an increase in believers during this time?

A: After Idi Amin, there was an increase because there was freedom. We began to construct churches made from papayas. Many of these papaya structures are still in Uganda today.

The church was gaining strength. Through the tough times people were coming to the church to get strength. The people's hope for the country was in God. They knew that the only safe place was to hide in God. So the number of Christians increased, even in Idi Amin's time.

Praise the Lord. That time prepared us for greater times to come. God is doing greater and mightier things today!

Whenever I am afraid,
I will trust in You.
In God (I will praise His word),
In God I have put my trust;
I will not fear,
What can flesh do to me?
Psalm 56: 3, 4

~ *Seven* ~

REWARDS OF OBEDIENCE

Jesus said to him, "If you can believe,
All things are possible to him who believes."
Mark 9:23

MAN'S BUSINESS RESTORED

A man came to me who was completely desperate. He said to me, "Pastor Steve, it has now been over one year and I do not have a job. I was a businessman, but I lost my business and went bankrupt. My family does not even have money to buy food. Sometimes we go without food for some days, drinking only water. Please, can you pray for me?"

I felt bad. You know that when people share with you such an experience you feel bad. And if you were able to do something to help them you would, because it is our duty.

I had no money, but I had Jesus, so I shared with him about Jesus. I opened my Bible and shared with him about the widow who came to the prophet Elisha. Her children were being sold as slaves because she had no money to pay her debts. She cried to the prophet and he asked her, "What shall I do for you? What do you have?"

She answered the prophet, "I don't have anything except a very little jar of oil." The man of God told her to go and borrow many vessels. He then told her, "Lock yourself in your house with your children and begin to pour out the oil." She did that and a miracle took place! As I shared that story with this gentleman, I encouraged him that the Lord God would perform a miracle for him.

This man had a building for his business, but it was now empty as he had closed his business the year before. As I prayed for him, the Lord very clearly told me, "Tell him to go and open his store tomorrow." So, I told him what the Lord had said.

He asked, "Even if I go and open my store, what shall I do next?"

I instructed him, "Tomorrow, go and open your store. Open it, sit there, and wait. The Lord will show you what to do next." So, he did that. In the morning, he woke up very early. He cleaned, swept, and made everything tidy. Then, he sat there. And, he sat and he sat.

As it was coming up to three o'clock in the afternoon, he saw a very big truck approaching his store. It was one of those very large trucks that carry a lot of tons. The truck came right up to his store and stopped. When the gentleman got out of the truck, he looked at him and realized that he knew him. This was the man whom he had dealt with in business ten years ago. His name was George.

George said, "My brother, how are you? I have a problem. Some people had ordered from me to supply them with cement, but now I don't have anywhere to take this cement and even more trucks are coming from Kenya."

This businessman had dealt in cement and hardware before his business had run bankrupt. And now George is asking him, "Please, can you take this cement? Please, don't mind about money. I will give you my bank account so that you can put the money into my bank account after you take off your profit. And if everything goes well, then all this cement will come to you. And, who knows? We may work together in more things after this."

This man could not believe what he was hearing. He was so happy! They unloaded the cement and from that time on his business came back to life. And even today, his business is going strong. That was a miracle from the Lord.

"At times we go through things in our lives and maybe we think that the Lord doesn't care. But, I tell you, my Friend out there, the Lord cares. The more you have suffered, I believe, the greater the victory you are going to get. Just hold on to Jesus. The victory is yours!" - Pastor Kaweesa

~*~*~

SENTONGO'S LIFE SPARED

We had a very poor brother who had lost his job and was living in a very bad situation. His name was Sentongo. Ever since he had lost his job from the East African community he had not received a good job. At this particular time he had no money at all. Some days his family went without food. Some days the sympathizers helped him with some little food.

There are some times when I don't sleep in my bed, but rather stay in my living room and pray and seek the face of the Lord by myself. This was one of those times when I had decided to seek the face of the Lord. As I was praying for various things the Lord brought a word to me and said, "Tomorrow, go and talk to Sentongo. He is planning to take a journey outside of the country to do business. Tell him he should <u>not</u> go on that trip. If he does, he is going to die and even the money is going to all be lost."

I was confused. Sentongo was very poor. He had no money. He was among the poorest in our church. I wondered, "Where did Sentongo get money? And, on top of that, where did he get the passport? He is poor. How did he work all that out?" But, I told the Lord, "Yes, Lord, I don't doubt you. You know best."

"Sometimes, my friends, the Lord brings His word right in the midst of a situation. The Lord will speak to you about what is going to happen. Like when He brought His word to the prophet Elisha, in the seventh chapter of second Kings, about the famine that had covered the whole country, telling him that the next day there would be much food. The king's servant didn't believe it, because it was beyond his imagination. He said, in verse two, "Even if God makes windows in heaven that kind of thing cannot happen."

There are times when God will bring His word in circumstances like that. I am so thankful that whenever the word of God comes, no matter how difficult the circumstances may be, the word of God changes everything. God's word is always true." - Pastor Kaweesa

The next day I went to the church for service. I didn't see Sentongo there, but his wife was there. So, after the service I told his wife everything that the Lord had told me.

She replied, "Do you know what? My husband left this morning and went to Tanzania". She then told me how he had gotten the money. "He got the money from his retirement when he had worked in the East Africa community, and he doesn't need a passport to go to Tanzania."

So, I said, "Okay, you go back to your house and pray and I will go to my house and pray. Let us pray that God will intervene miraculously."

When she returned to her house, she found that Sentongo had not gone to Tanzania after all. She asked him why. He told her that the ferry he was to take from Uganda to Tanzania across Lake Victoria had been delayed. He said that he would go the next day.

His wife then told him, "Before you go, Pastor Kaweesa has a word from the Lord for you concerning that journey." He asked her what the message was, but she told him to go and find out in the morning before he left on his trip. He was very anxious to find out what the Lord was saying about his journey.

He came very early in the morning and sat in my living room. I told him, "The Lord has said to tell you to not go on the trip to Tanzania to do business. If you go you are going to die and your money is going to be lost. So, you must not go."

He asked me, "Pastor Kaweesa, can't we pray that God may change?"

I answered him, "There are some things we can pray about that God changes. I have seen that happen many times. However, in this situation, the only thing for you to do is to stay. If you stay you are going to live, but if you go you are going to die."

He put his head down and said, "Pastor, I am not going. But, I don't know how to explain this to my friend who was taking me."

He went and told his friend that he was not going to Tanzania, that God had told him not to go. His friend, who was Catholic, was very confused and asked, "God told you not to go? God spoke to you? Can God come and speak to you? Does He not only speak through the Pope?" He continued, "Don't lie. God does not come and speak to people. That is your imagination." However, even though there was a disagreement, he did not go either.

Three days later, the very ferry that Sentongo and his friend would have been on to return home, capsized and killed over a thousand people. You may have read about it in the newspaper. Rescuers failed to even retrieve all of the bodies; they were only able to recover about one hundred bodies from the surface. If I remember correctly, this happened in about 1995. You can check the story out from the old papers.

So, I tell you what, the man who was not born-again was the first one to read about that accident in the newspaper. He came trembling to Sentongo and said, "Sentongo, your God is the Living God. Your God is the real God. If you had not warned me I would have been dead today." He was shedding tears as he said, "Today, I am accepting your God." He was very thankful to God.

Sentongo also glorified God. He realized that God really loved him regardless of all the difficulties he had gone through of not having a job, of lacking money, of not having enough food. He wondered why God had chosen to save him out of that thousand people. He said, "Out of all that thousand people, I am not the best." He was very, very thankful.

God had a plan for Sentongo. He is now the pastor of our prison ministries. We are currently ministering at twenty-five prisons in the district of Masaka and in the district of Sembabule. This man and his wife are doing a great, great job. Every month, they have an average of eighty prisoners who get born-again.

If we had lost this man, my, you can imagine what would have happened. God had a plan for Sentongo. And, maybe Satan said, "Let me kill this man, because, what he is going to do in the future is so big and so great that I cannot stomach it. Let me try to kill him."

Sentongo was spared. We were so thankful. And, even today, when we see what is going on in our prisons, we give glory to the Almighty God.

"God speaks to His people. The gifts of the Spirit are still alive today. God is still the same today as yesterday. When God speaks, just obey what He is saying. If you will obey, you will be blessed. You will see the mighty hand of God move." - Pastor Kaweesa

~*~*~

UNEDUCATED WOMAN READS HER BIBLE

I was in a meeting, when a lady came to me and said, "Pastor, I admit, I did not go to school. I do not know how to read. I do not know how to write. It hurts me that as they preach to me, I cannot read my Bible. Can you help me? Can you pray for me that God may teach me?" She was very serious. As she shared with me, she was close to shedding tears. I sympathized with her.

I thought that the only way one could learn to read was by going to school. However, in this instance, this lady was in her fifties and I did not know of any school that would teach older people to read and write. So, I encouraged her to believe for a miracle to be performed in her life.

I laid my hands upon her and prayed, "Good Lord, it is You who teaches people to read and write. Even though there are schools, this lady did not have an opportunity to go to school. Lord, You have a miracle for her. I pray that You will perform a miracle for her."

I prayed the prayer that Isaiah prayed in Isaiah, chapter fifty. I said, "Lord, give this lady the language of the learned. Open her hands that when she gets a pen, she may be able to write. Lord, help her to understand letters." That is what I prayed.

This lady took that very serious. I was serious also, but I think that she was more serious than I. She had faith. She went back believing and thanking God. Have you ever prayed for people and you find out that they have more faith than you do? That's what has happened to me. Such people have helped me to rise up in faith.

When she got home she told her children, "Do you know what? The Lord, from today, has taught me how to read and how to write. I am going to read my Bible and I am going to write." So, the children brought the Bible to her and opened it. She could not read it. But, she said, "Yes. I have learned how to read. You shall see in time."

That night she slept. And in way past sleep, she received a dream. In this dream she saw a Bible. A hand was holding the Bible. As the hand was holding the Bible a mighty wind came. This wind started to open every page in that Bible. The pages were flapping as the wind was opening them at a very high speed. This lady was watching the dream, after which, she heard a voice say to her, "Now, you know how to read. Get your Bible and start reading."

She woke up! She jumped! She exclaimed, "Oh, my! I can read!" She got her Bible and miraculously she was able to read her Bible! She praised and glorified the name of the Living God! God is a God of miracles.

"God performs miracles. Who thinks that God does not perform miracles? God performs miracles! I want to encourage you that God is able to perform a miracle in your life!

There is room for a miracle in your life." - Pastor Kaweesa

~*~*~

GRACE TO FACE A COBRA

Lake Victoria has about eighty-five islands. The Lord called us to start a church on one of the islands named Lwaje Island. The way we got the island was through one of our hospital ministries. As our people were ministering in the hospitals in Uganda, they ministered to a lady who said, "Please, can you bring this Good News to our place?" So, they took the address of the island. We had never been there before.

Lwaje Island is about five miles long and three miles wide. Pastor Stephen Mayanga, Pastor Ron DeVore and I went and surveyed the island. This island was a bush land and had never been disturbed all these years. The people there are fishermen and live right on the shores of the island near the water.

There was no single church on the island, no single school, no single hospital, not even a clinic. Can you imagine how people were living? People there on the island, even today, are still having those kinds of troubles and suffering.

We told the people on the island what we wanted to do and they welcomed us with two open arms. We arranged and conducted a crusade there and a church was planted. Sometime later I went back there myself to stay with the pastor whom we had sent there. His name is Fred Musoke.

Pastor Musoke was living in a small hut. It's completely jungle where we planted the church. And this jungle, it had, oh my, it had snakes and snakes and snakes. Pastor Musoke told me story after story. Every time he went out from his hut to get something, like to buy food, when he came back, he found a snake. He had fought snakes and snakes and snakes.

So, during that week as I was visiting, we visited one of the villages near the water. Later that evening we were walking back home down the trail at about eight o'clock in the night. The batteries in the flashlight we had were a bit low, so my brother was leading and I was following after him.

He heard something and he jumped. When I looked down, oh my God, there was a cobra. It had turned itself around. When a cobra is ready to bite, what it does is it turns itself around. It turns on its back and it raises its head. It was preparing to get me right on my leg!

I jumped and shouted, "Jesus!" Cobras are very stubborn snakes. They don't run. This snake stayed right there, so we got stones and hit it. God gave us the grace. We overpowered it and we killed that cobra.

I took the skin off of the snake. I took it to my church to show them what our brother is going through and what the people who go to Lwaje Island go through. Everyone who saw the skin was very thankful to God that He had saved us from that kind of death. If we had been bitten, we would have died because there is no hospital, there is nothing.

~*~*~

OBEDIENCE IS BETTER

We have a group called the "Born-Again Married Group". This group consists of married people from different churches. We formed this group to encourage people in their marriages. We counsel them, talk to them, hold seminars and visit their homes. We have done this for quite a few years. We also encourage members to recruit new members.

One brother recruited a new member. I did not know this new member or what was taking place in his home, but I went to visit him. He lived in a very poor, small house that was still under construction.

As usual, we sing and share the word of the Lord. So, we sang, we prayed, and then they asked me to give the word of the Lord. As I was opening my Bible to share a scripture, I heard the voice of the Lord say, "What I tell you to say, say that."

I said, "Yes, Lord. Go ahead, my Father."

The Lord went on to tell me, "Ask that brother if he is still doing the work which I called him to do." So, I asked him that.

This brother, who was named Brother Sengendo, answered, "No."

The Lord continued, "Tell him that unless he will answer the call I have placed on his life, he will never see any blessing. He will not succeed in life. And, he must be very careful for if he does not change his days are numbered." I was afraid upon hearing that. I shared with him, and his wife started shedding tears.

I felt so bad. I inquired of him, "Brother Sengendo, please tell us what went wrong. Why did you forsake the ministry? Tell us what you were doing in God's ministry."

This brother told us, "Yes, it's true, I was a minister. I was a pastor. I was serving in a church in a very difficult village. The church was very difficult for me. The main reason that I forsook that church was that a time came when I could not feed my family. I could not help my children, so I left the church."

I asked him, "When you decided to leave the church, did you endeavor to get a replacement and leave a pastor to that flock?"

He answered, "No. I was very frustrated. I told the Christians, 'I am leaving, but you, among yourselves, choose someone who will help you out.' Then I left."

I told this brother, "You did wrong. It would have been okay for you to leave, but you would have needed to make sure that you left a pastor in the church before you could go. You left the flock without a shepherd."

He went on to say that when he left the church, he had come to this town to look for jobs. This had been about five years ago. I asked him, "Are you now able to help the family and feed the family?"

He said, "Please, no. I am doing a very, very poor job. I have three children. I have failed to pay the school fees of the two children, and for one child a good sympathizer is helping me out." When he spoke that, everyone went down in tears. We cried and cried. We were very sorry for this pastor.

I then spoke the word of the Lord to encourage him. We prayed for his call. He had a call. He just needed to rekindle that call. I asked him which church he was attending, but he didn't even have a church or pastor. I knew he was in very great trouble.

I encouraged him to find a pastor, to introduce himself to that pastor, and explain everything. I said, "I believe that pastor will be able to help you." We then left.

Within me, the Lord showed me that Brother Sengendo had not changed. I began to pray for him everyday. I desired that the Lord would help him out of that trouble. But, within four months, he died of a stroke. I felt so bad. I couldn't understand it. I couldn't explain it.

"What I want to say, is that the Lord warned that man. God gave him a chance, but he didn't use that opportunity at all.

Please, any ministers out there, if you run into trouble like that, please don't run away. If you are a pastor, evangelist or an elder, don't just run away from problems. There is a better way to handle it. We can't just run away from our problems.

Stand and wait on the Lord. Call on the name of the Lord and seek His advice and guidance in that kind of problem or trouble. The good Lord will send you His help; He will come and handle your problem.

Don't just run away. Don't run from church to church. That's not right. God has called you to a particular church. If you are a pastor, God has called you to serve Him in a particular church. Be there. Let God solve the problems. Don't just run away. Don't resign. That's not God. I don't believe that God does things that way.

Jesus faced many problems, but in every problem, there was victory for Him. There is victory for you as you wait on the Lord. Please, don't just run away and forsake the flock of the Lord. Those people are precious to God; those Christians are God's people. God has put you there for a purpose, you are serving Him. It is not a man who called you, it is God who called you. So, serve God who called you. In problems, call upon the name of the Living God."
– Pastor Kaweesa

~*~*~

TRUST AND OBEY: IT'S THE BEST WAY

Anet is a daughter of our Brother and Sister Mubiri. They are very active members in our church. After Anet finished high school, it was time for her to join her college schooling. She, along with her parents, chose a catering college in Kampala which was headed by the late Mr. Sekasi. After getting all the college forms and looking for all the money which was needed, she was left with only a short time before her school was to start.

One day Anet came to my office for prayer. She was sick of a fever. As I was about to pray, I felt within my spirit to ask her about what she was doing. She told me how she would soon join a catering school. As she was telling me all that, the Lord told me that she was not to join that school, but instead she was to join a nursing school.

Within my spirit I prayed and prayed for God's wisdom to share with this young girl to help her do what the Lord wanted her to do. I told her, "Anet, the course of catering you want to take is good, but in your case the Lord has spoken to me that you are to join a nursing college." She started crying and I felt that maybe I had told her something that she hated. In that moment I was wondering what I should say next. I prayed, "Lord, help me. This is your daughter."

"Friend, what I have learned is that when the Lord gives me a word of knowledge to give to people I pray for God's wisdom in how to share that. Because, I understand

that the Lord gives such a word to lift that person up so that he or she may come close to the Lord. Doing it this way has worked for me during my twenty-nine years of ministry." - Pastor Kaweesa

Anet then told me that she was crying because of joy! The first thing that she wanted to do in her life was to be a nurse. However, because she didn't get very good points in high school, she didn't want to take a course that she wouldn't be able to finish. Therefore, she discussed it with her parents and then changed to catering which they thought would be an easier course.

God knows our weak points and He is there to give us strength. She told me, "Pastor Steven, now I know that I can do it! And I am going to tell my parents what the Lord wants me to do." She went and told her parents what the Lord wanted for her. They agreed. So, after changing the course and the college, she joined a nursing school.

After six months, Anet got some shocking news about the college that she had planned to join to take the catering course. The head of the college, Mr. Sekasi, along with his students, had gone for a tour of the game park in the north of our country. As they were taking a tour to see the animals, the Lord's Resistance Army, (the LRA Rebels), ambushed them and over ten students were killed, together with Mr. Sekasi and a young girl from our village of Seguku.

It was a big shock to Anet, but also, she marveled at how the Lord loved her so much that He had stopped her from joining that college. This testimony, along with a number of other testimonies from those who I have given

God's Word, puts me in a place where I never take God's Word cheap.

As I am writing, Anet has finished her nursing course and she works in one of the clinics around Kampala. She has told me that she is very happy with her job.

Trust in the Lord with all your heart,
and lean not on your own understanding;
In all your ways acknowledge Him,
and He shall direct your paths.
Proverbs 3: 5, 6

~ Eight ~

SIGNS AND WONDERS

No evil shall befall you,
nor shall any plague come near your dwelling;
For He shall give His angels charge over you,
to keep you in all your ways.
Psalm 91: 10 – 11

Steven Kaweesa

ANGEL'S SONGS REFRESH ME

I was walking five miles to go to school. While I was in school I had also started ministering. Each week we fasted three days and three nights. This was during the time when the church was being persecuted. We felt that we had to do something in order for God to hear our prayers because of the scripture:

If my people who are called by My name
will humble themselves,
and pray and seek My face,
and turn from their wicked ways,
then I will hear from heaven,
And I will forgive their sin and heal their land.
2 Chronicles 7:14

As I was walking home on the third day of my fast I felt very, very tired. There was a hill which I had to go over to reach my home. I was very weak and was praying in my heart, "Jesus, I love you. Jesus, give me strength. Jesus, continue to help me."

Suddenly, I saw a very large group of angels. They were singing a wonderful and beautiful song which caused all my weakness, exhaustion, and all the hunger that I was feeling to disappear. It was a very beautiful and great experience.

The angels sang and sang. I was just praising the Lord within my spirit. I didn't want to disturb this kind of experience. I walked that whole mile with the angels singing. I heard them singing audibly. When I reached my door the angels disappeared. I was so thankful to the Lord. I shared that kind of experience with my Auntie whom I was living with at the time, as well as my fellow cousins. We all praised the Living God!

That whole night I did not sleep. It was so marvelous, so great! Angels are real. Angels are present. That experience assured me that although I don't see them daily, they are always there to guard and take care of me. That is their duty. The Lord promised us in Psalm 91 that He will give His angels charge over us to keep us in all our ways.

"What I have learned is that angels are here to minister to us whether we see them or not. I remember one night when Ron and Shirley DeVore were returning back to their home after a visit. It was dark and here in Uganda when it gets dark, it is very dark. Their way was dark as they were walking through a small, narrow pass. Suddenly, an angel of the Lord came and led them up to their home!" - Pastor Kaweesa

~*~*~

ANGELS PRAISE GOD

Another time, I was on a three-day fast. It was the second day at about ten o'clock at night. I had been reading my Bible.

I had a small African drum and began to praise the Lord. I was beating the drum and praising and praising. I felt so good as I was praising the Living God. I praised for about two hours and then felt that I was a bit tired and sleepy so I put the drum aside and tried to lie down. Whenever I was fasting and praying I would just lie on a mat, not on a mattress. Lying on a mat would help wake me up more often to pray, because that is what I was doing, fasting and praying.

I put the drum aside and I lay down. But then, I heard the same rhythm in the drum. I woke up and was at first a bit afraid. I wondered, "What is taking place?" However, then I was encouraged, because I knew that a demon could not beat the drum in such a way for praising the Lord. I thought, "You know, maybe the Lord has sent the angels and now they are drumming." I didn't see the angels, but the drumming was going on.

I stood up and started clapping my hands. I danced and danced and danced until the time came that I was tired. I sat down and then slowly by slowly, sleep took me away. I slept.

I knew that God gave me that experience to show me that He is on my side. In those days, we were often praying and seeking the face of God for our very lives. The devil had been attacking us with fear that we would be killed. That kind of experience strengthened me knowing that God is on my side, He is with me. The devil can do nothing about it. I was very thankful to God.

But he himself went on a day's journey into the wilderness,
and came and sat down under a juniper tree.
And he prayed that he might die, and said,
"It is enough! Now, Lord, take my life,
for I am no better than my fathers!"
Then as he lay and slept under a juniper tree,

*suddenly an angel touched him, and said to him,
"Arise and eat." Then he looked and by his head
was a cake baked on coals, and a jar of water.
So he ate and drank and lay down again.
And the angel of the Lord came back a second time,
and touched him and said,
"Arise and eat because the journey
is too great for you." 1 Kings 19: 4 – 7*

~*~*~

CROWN ON PASTOR'S HEAD

As we were having an "over-night" meeting during Idi Amin's time and the underground church, we were praising and glorifying the name of the Lord. We worshiped with praising, dancing, clapping, praying and sharing the word of the Lord.

Three ladies who visited that meeting were not born-again. At the end of the service when we had dismissed the congregation those ladies came to me and told me that they wanted to become born-again. In those times, even if one, two or three wanted to become born-again it was a very, very, great, great miracle! We thanked God so much! We knew that during those times he or she may die at anytime. So, I was very, very happy with their decision.

As I was sharing with them about the saving power of Jesus Christ, one lady interrupted me, "Pastor, before you continue, can we ask you a question?" I answered her, "Yes, please, go ahead."

She then asked me, "What was on your head when you started preaching?"

"What was on my head when I started preaching?" I asked.

She explained to me, "Yes, when you stood up to preach, a very big crown came on your head. It had many colors, many beautiful colors. And they were very bright. As you preached the brightness continued to grow brighter. I was the first to see it and then I asked my two sisters if they saw it. Both of them saw it, also. All three of us saw the crown! It stayed on you until you told us to pray at which time we closed our eyes. When we opened our eyes the crown was gone. What does that crown mean?"

Within my spirit, I asked, "Lord, what was that?" Earlier that night as I had come to the meeting from home I had felt very, very weak. I was disturbed and so much afraid. I had felt that I was going to die, but I had come anyway to the night service. When those ladies told me that story I was amazed and happy.

I tried to answer the question which she had asked me. I said, "The Jesus that you are accepting today has life for you in this present life and He also has life for you in the time to come. So, when you are gone out of this world there will be wonderful crowns which each one of you is going to receive. The Lord just wanted you to know that if you accept Him the crown which you saw on my head is the same crown you are going to have."

So, they were very happy and thankful to God. They accepted the Lord as I led them in a prayer of welcoming

Jesus into their life. They were totally and completely born-again.

Finally, there is laid up for me
the crown of righteousness,
which the Lord, the righteous Judge,
will give to me on that Day,
and not to me only but also to
all who have loved His appearing.
2 Timothy 4:8

~*~

Behold, I am coming quickly!
Hold fast what you have,
that no one may take your crown.
Revelation 3: 11

~*~*~

WITCH DOCTOR SERVES POISON JUICE

We were conducting a crusade in about 1983 that was way out on the east side of our country in a place called Soroti. We had seminars in the mornings and in the evenings we held the crusade. Hundreds of people turned out for this crusade.

A very strong witchdoctor had come for our meetings and he seemed to become saved. He had confessed to receive Jesus. Everyone was so happy! And yet, he was only lying and deceiving us. What he wanted to do was to try and kill us. Let me tell you the whole story.

That witchdoctor invited the pastors of the crusade to his house. The pastors said, "Oh, praise the Lord! Let us go to his house. Who knows? Maybe the wife and the children will all get born again, also!" So, we went praising. We had just finished the day's crusade where many had received Jesus Christ. What a wonderful time! We were all very, very happy and talking about all that the Lord had done.

As we arrived at this man's house, he met us with some juice he had specially prepared for us. We wanted that juice very badly as it had been a long, hot day. During those years in Uganda all the factories were completely shut down and you did not see any bottles of soda, no sodas of any kind. Almost all of the factories had been closed because of the many wars. We had almost gone back to the Stone Ages!

People would prepare their own juice from passion fruit or some other fruit. So, that's what this witchdoctor had done for us and we were so thankful. As we drank the juice we continued talking about Jesus and witnessing to those that were around us. After we had finished drinking the juice none of us felt anything. We left and went back to the place where we were being housed.

Then, the witchdoctor, who we thought had been born again, boasted to his friends, saying, "Now, I have finished them! They came into this area trying to steal my people! They have tried to deceive us by bringing their Jesus. I have finished them now! They are going to die!" He had taken poison and put it into our juice!

But, I tell you, God is so wonderful. God is so good. God is so great. The Lord promised us in Mark 16 that if we should drink any deadly thing, we shall not be hurt. That is exactly what took place. Not one of us fell sick. None of us had any tummy problem. Not one of us felt any kind of disturbance in our bodies. We were completely fine and continued with the seven-day crusade. Those who had heard about that incident came to the crusade wanting to confirm if we were going to die or stay alive. We drank the poison juice on the third day of the crusade. We continued and nothing happened to us.

After we finished the crusade we left the area and never saw the witchdoctor again. However, this incident brought many people to Jesus Christ. People realized that you do not joke or play with the Born-agains. They said, "They have their God and you better be careful!"

God had once again spared our lives. When you serve God, He will never forsake you. He is going to be with you all the time. What He promised is always true.

And, these signs will follow those who believe:
In My name they will cast out demons;
they will speak with new tongues;
they will take up serpents;
and if they drink any deadly thing,
it will by no means hurt them;
they will lay hands on the sick,
and they will recover.
Mark 16: 17 – 18

~*~*~

"In First Kings, chapter eighteen, verses twenty through forty, Elijah got a wonderful, great victory. Israel turned back to their God.

Fire came down from heaven and consumed the burnt sacrifice. All the prophets of Baal were killed; not one of them escaped. Elijah killed them all by himself. This was great! Everyone who was there on the mountain feared the Lord, even King Ahab.

Ahab told Jezebel all that Elijah had done and how he had slain all the prophets with the sword. Jezebel then sent a messenger to Elijah, saying, "So let the gods do to me, and more also, if I do not make your life as one of them by tomorrow about this time." (1 Kings 19:1-2) In all this, the devil did not give up. He was planning an attack on the life of Elijah.

Let me say this to you, my friend, the devil has not given up on you. In times of great victory the enemy may be planning an attack. But, I tell you what, the Lord is on <u>your</u> side! The great God you have believed in is there to give you more and more victory!" - Pastor Kaweesa

Now thanks be to God,
Who always leads us in triumph in Christ,
and through us manifests the fragrance of his
knowledge in every place.
2 Corinthians 2:14

~ *Nine* ~

WITCHDOCTORS, CANNIBALISM AND NIGHT DANCING . . . . . . ONLY A MYTH?

And when He had called His twelve
disciples to Him, He gave them power
over unclean spirits, to cast them out,
and to heal all kinds of sickness,
and all kinds of disease.
Matthew 10:1

111

WITCHDOCTOR TURNS TO JESUS

There was a witchdoctor in a certain village where we were preaching in the early 1980s. This witchdoctor heard the gospel, came to us and asked a question, "Can Jesus really help me? I am a witchdoctor. I know that I have bewitched a number of people and many people have died as a result of my witchcraft. Can God forgive me? Can God love me, a person like myself who has tormented people and done a lot of harm?"

I answered him, "Yes. Jesus came to save the sinners. Jesus has a place for you. And, Jesus loves you."

Then, he asked, "What about the people I have killed?"

I told him, "If today, you believe in Jesus Christ, no matter how big your sins are, He will forgive you. Repent, and turn to Him totally with all your heart." I also told him, "We will have to burn your shrine and all the witchcraft that you have."

Then he said, "I am so afraid of that witchcraft, because sometimes they even threaten to kill me. There are times they do not allow me to sleep on my bed. There are times they do not allow me to eat. There are times they even tell me to stay outside. I live in fear. If I burn up the shrine, am I going to be safe? Won't those spirits turn against me and kill me?"

I opened up the scriptures and showed him about the wonderful things that Jesus did for people when He cast out powerful demons. I encouraged this man that Jesus loves him and has enough power. I assured him that there is no power on the earth, above the earth, or beneath the earth which is above the name of Jesus Christ.

With those words, this witchdoctor was encouraged and he accepted Jesus. He then led us to his house. When we reached there we saw a large shrine. In the shrine he had all kinds of odd stuff. We surrounded the shrine and prayed in the name of Jesus. We sang some songs. We praised the Lord. A very large group of Christians had gathered.

We then told this young man to bring a fire, which he did, and we lit his shrine with fire. And oh, my God, the shrine began burning, and it burned and burned and burned. Everything completely burned to ashes.

That man knelt down and gave his life to Jesus Christ. He was crying and shedding tears. The tears were not because he was afraid, but rather the tears were from how happy he was. He had been trapped in a life where he didn't believe that anyone could help him come out of that kind of misery. He was totally and completely freed.

We went back to our homes praising the Lord because that was a very, very big testimony to that village as well as to other villages. It was a great testimony to all the people that came to that shrine. Some of the people were disappointed, but many were very, very happy for they had lived in fear of this witchdoctor and his death threats. Now that he had turned to Jesus, people knew that he would no longer hurt them again. So, most of the people in the village were happy.

We thanked Jesus.

...Though your sins are like scarlet,
they shall be as white as snow;
Though they are red like crimson,
they shall be as wool.
Isaiah 1:18

"Friend, those who have not accepted Jesus Christ fear the witchdoctors. So, if they see such a witchdoctor burning his shrine and turning to Jesus Christ and making Him their Lord, some people are a bit happy, while others are a bit confused. They wonder, "Is that man going to make it? Won't those evil spirits come back and kill him?"

But, generally, the people of the village are very happy because they know that the witchdoctors bewitch people and send evil spirits to certain people. The evil spirits go to them and disturb them. And, in the end, the tormented people go to these very same witchdoctors and consult with them and are then required to give them a lot of money." - Pastor Kaweesa

~*~*~

PARENTS SEEK HELP FROM WITCHDOCTOR

A young girl became born-again. We baptized her. She loved the Lord very, very much. However, a time came when she fell sick. Her family was very strong believing in witchcraft and witchdoctors. They told their daughter, "We are taking you to our witchdoctor. You have no choice. Take away your Jesus. Jesus is a lie. Why did you fall sick?"

This young girl was weak and could do nothing. She was taken away from us about thirty miles. There was no telephone, nothing. And we did not know what kind of situation was taking place to our sister as her family took her to the witchdoctor. The witchdoctor they had taken her to had a shrine way deep in the forest. It was about two to three miles from the main road and surrounded by jungle. The only way to get there was by foot. After about a month we got news of what had happened to this young sister. Another pastor and I went right to that shrine.

"My Friend, people are very disturbed and troubled in this world. The devil is very foolish. You cannot believe what the devil does to people. We must preach the Gospel! We must believe in demon casting. We must believe in Jesus Christ and His atoning Blood!" - Pastor Kaweesa

We reached the shrine and to our amazement, we saw something which we had never seen in this world! Over a hundred people, including men, women, and children, were on the shrine in the midst of the jungle. The witchdoctor was deceiving all those people! He had fooled them into believing that he is going to heal them. That is how the witchdoctors fool people and steal from them, even the little that they have. They steal away their chickens, goats, cows, and clothes.

We found our sister and asked her, "Are you for Jesus? Or, are you for the devil?"

This sister was very weak, but she answered, "My brothers, my pastors, I am for Jesus. It is my mom and my dad that have brought me to this place. I hate this place. I told them time and again that I do not want this place and to take me back to my pastor. They refused."

We asked her, "Do you have any belongings here?"

She answered us, "No, only the clothes I am in." So, we got hold of her, one on each side, and we walked away.

The witchdoctor shouted to her as we left, "If you die, I will not bury you! Do not ever come back to me!"

We told him, "She will not come back to you. You are not her savior. This girl belongs to the Almighty God." And, we went on our way. This girl's mother looked on thinking that we were going to die there on our way, but to her surprise we went away with our sister victoriously.

Our sister was very, very happy. She praised and glorified the name of the Lord. We took her to a medical place in Seguku where they treated her. And, although we prayed for her, the sickness had gone far and the Lord did not allow her to live. After about six months she died. She had been suffering from AIDS.

After she died, the mother and dad heard about it and came to us. They said, "Please, help us. We did foolishly. We did not know what to do. Pray for us."

We took this sister to her home and we buried her. There was a very strong testimony and preaching of the Word of the Lord. People got
born-again, including her mother and father. They both gave their lives to the Lord on the day of their daughter's burial.

The Lord told us to go and rescue our sister from the hand of the devil and that's what we did. Please do what the Lord is telling you to do.

~*~*~

SHOWDOWN!

Some of my fellow ministers, led by Elder Musitwa Joseph, went down to a village to hold a crusade and preach the Gospel. People were getting born-again, people were getting healed, and people were getting delivered.

On about the third day, a witchdoctor came and spoke to the brother who was running the crusade, saying, "Since the time you came I have heard what your Jesus can do. I have heard that your Jesus is very powerful. I want to challenge you and so I set this challenge before you: I want you to send your Jesus to me and I will send my demonic forces to you. And, as I send these demonic forces to you, I want them to kill you. And, I challenge your Jesus to come and kill me."

But, the minister of the gospel said, "Our Jesus did not come to this village to kill people. Our Jesus came to this village to save people, even you. You are included if you will open up your heart and accept Jesus Christ."

The witchdoctor declared, "I want nothing to do with your Jesus! I only want to challenge you. I want you to show me that kind of power. Allow me to send my demonic forces. And, if you don't die, if you are spared, then I will know that your Jesus is the most powerful and I will accept him." So, the challenge was put forth.

This certain witchdoctor was greatly feared in the village. The people knew what he had done and how he had killed people. They knew how he had bewitched people and given out witchcraft, and with that witchcraft, a lot of harm had been done to their fellow people. As the witchdoctor put forth the challenge many people began screaming, especially those who hated the Born-agains shouted, "We shall see! We shall see about your Jesus!"

The ministers of God told the man, "You go ahead. Go ahead and send your demons. We don't fear them; the Lord has not given us the spirit of fear. But, if you don't accept our Lord you will be in trouble."

Following the crusade that day our fellow ministers went back home. After finishing a crusade here in Africa we may praise, we may dance, and we may jump and shout showing our thanks to the Lord. Then, we eat and share and share and share. Sometimes we may go into the middle of the night.

And, so it happened, in the middle of the night a large group of motorcycles came. Then, someone was shaking the side of the house. The Born-agains knew that the demonic forces had come so they prayed, "We command you, demonic forces, to go back to the very person who sent you here. But, don't kill him, in Jesus' name. Be gone!" They then heard the motorcycles turn around and leave. (The devil has some limited power he can loose on sound to be heard. But, do you know what? The Lord has all the power!)

In the morning when the Born-agains reached the witchdoctor's house, they saw what the evil spirits had done. The roof was taken off of his house and had been thrown almost one mile away! This man also had a large garden on about four acres of land. He had trees of bananas, and also coffee trees. Those evil spirits had uprooted every tree of coffee and every banana tree.

That morning the whole village saw his house without a roof and his plantation completely destroyed. He got his belongings together, along with his wife and children, and ran away from the village. That village was never the same. People walked miles to come to the crusade when they heard what the Lord had done to that witchdoctor. It was a very powerful crusade, and by the end of the night, many, many people had turned to Jesus Christ.

~*~*~

"Sometimes I have seen it here in Africa, and it may be in other countries, especially where the demonic operation is very heavy, that when the people see the power of God, they think that the ministers have extra demonic powers. Some from the village thought that these ministers were very great witchdoctors, very powerful witchdoctors.

The devil is a liar. He brings all kinds of lies to the people. But, people can overcome these kinds of lies as they stand on the Word of the Lord.

We have seen many people come and listen to the word of God with their hearts wide, wide open. They ask, "Who is this Jesus who can do such marvelous, powerful things?" - Pastor Kaweesa

~*~*~

WITCHDOCTOR FLEES VILLAGE

One night as we were conducting an all night prayer meeting, at Mr. Sakku's home in Gaba near Kampala, a witchdoctor came. His heart was very, very hard. He did not come to listen to the Word of God, but rather came thinking that he would bewitch the Born-agains and confuse our meeting. However, the meeting went on and there was no disruption as we preached the word of God that night. Some, who had come not born-again, became born-again in that overnight meeting.

The witchdoctor went back to his home and entered his shrine. He tried to do his witchcraft and check on his demons, but they were nowhere to be found. They had run away. He sensed it. He knew what had happened and he was so much afraid.

That day, the witchdoctor who had disturbed that village for so long, ran away from the village. No one knew where he went. A great number of people then came to know the Lord as their personal Savior and Lord.

"My Brother and Sister, many times witchdoctors have tried to rise up against us during our outreaches. But, time after time, the Lord has shamed them. We have seen the witchdoctor's followers give their lives to the Lord. And, as I am writing now, we are seeing more and more witchdoctors coming to the Lord." - Pastor Kaweesa

~*~*~

PARENTS GIVE DAUGHTER TO WITCHDOCTOR

We were in a night service with about one hundred people in the early 1980's at Kabowa Redeemed Church. As we were praising and worshiping God a woman started screaming and throwing her arms around. Anyone who was near her was beaten by her arms. I rose up with some other colleagues and we got a hold of her.

In a very terrible voice, she said, "You are joking with others, but not with me. I am strong and I am going to defeat you! This is my lady! Why did she come in this church? I have married this lady since she was three years old!"

In Jesus' name, we took that woman out of the congregation to the office, where we rebuked the evil spirits. They declared, "We have married this lady! She is ours. Leave us alone! You have many other people. Why don't you go ahead with those people? Why are you disturbing us? You are giving us a very hard time. Now you are trying to take all of our people." The demons were crying and begging for mercy as they said, "Let us go! Let us go!" We prayed and cast them out in Jesus' name. The lady was totally and completely delivered.

After she was delivered she told us how it came about that she acquired those spirits. She said that when she was born her parents were very much used in the witchcraft. So, they took her to the witchdoctor and he told her parents that the spirits had said that they wanted to marry their daughter. The parents accepted that and they left that young girl to grow up at the witchdoctor's shrine.

This young girl had worked in the shrine and traveled with the witchdoctor. She was the one going and preparing those harbs for the people who would frequent the shrine. (As I explained to you earlier, *harbs* are made up of roots, parts of bats, and other things considered "spiritual".)

The witchdoctor began sleeping with her at a very, very early age. She could not even remember when. She did not know how to read or write. When she was about twenty-five years old, she met someone and told them of her many years of suffering. The lady she met told her, "What I can do is to take you to the Born-agains." So, she had escaped from the shrine and had come with this lady to our meeting.

We shared with her about the love of Jesus Christ and we told her that she was now totally and completely free from that demonic possession. She accepted Christ and said that she would never go back to that witchdoctor. For many years she came to our church. She loves the Living God.

"The Lord died and took every person's sin. No matter where you come from, or what color or nationality you are, the Lord loves you. He came to save you and give you life." - Pastor Kaweesa

~*~*~

Writer's word of warning: *Due to the disturbing content, the remainder of this chapter may not be suitable for children. This testimony has been included as told by Pastor*

Kaweesa. The following are stories from his experiences with the real-life bondages of cannibalism in his country of Uganda.

CANNIBALISM . . . DOES IS STILL EXIST?

A minister friend of mine, whom I had ministered with in a number of meetings, was ministering way down deep in the villages. As he was conducting a revival meeting in a certain church a family came and said, "We want to get born-again, but we have a problem."

The minister asked, "What kind of problem?"

They answered, "We are night dancing."

The minister shared with them, "Even the night dancer gets born-again." But, this family still believed that their situation was very, very difficult. The minister asked them, "Why? Why is it so tough? There is no tough situation which God cannot solve."

This minister had heard about night dancing, but he was not sure whether all the stories he had heard were true, like eating dead bodies. Soon, however, he was going to find out.

The family further explained, "We have a problem, that even up to now, we have this meat, human meat. What can we do with it?" The minister told them, in Jesus' name, to go and get it. So, they went to their home and brought back all the human meat.

Now, the minister did not want to show to the congregation that he was a bit scared, but he was very scared. However, he received encouragement from the

Lord and he prayed for the family. The demonic possession ran out from them and they were completely and totally delivered. This family gave their lives to the Lord.

~*~*~

"Friend, what I can say, is that I have seen a number of strange kinds of demonic attacks. They are of the enemy. This type of demonic possession is real. I have seen some strong, strong demonic forces and have confronted them. I have prayed for people with them. And, I have seen the power of God deliver them. So, even with those terrible evil spirits of night dancing, when a person gets born-again, that person will be completely freed.

Some people don't believe that such spirits are real. But, I can tell you this, that a person's unbelief doesn't take away the truth. When the Lord gave us power to cast out demonic forces, He knew that even these kinds of demonic forces of night dancing are real." - Pastor Kaweesa

~*~*~

WOMAN DELIVERED FROM NIGHT DANCING

One lady came that was disturbed by the spirit of cannibalism, the spirit of night dancing, and the spirit of eating the dead. She came and shared this with me and explained to me how she had been given this problem when she was very, very little. Her parents had cut her and put witchcraft in her. She then found that she was night dancing.

It is my duty and obligation to share with these people Jesus Christ. I shared at great lengths with this lady, after which I prayed for her. She then began screaming and crawling on the floor. I prayed for an hour and it did not seem that she was going to get free. I began to get a little tired, but continued to pray. Her situation took almost eight hours.

No matter how long a situation takes, I have seen deliverance. She was totally and completely set free.

~*~*~

WITCHCRAFT PLANTED IN YOUNG GIRL

Another lady also came to my office and when I asked her why she had come she started becoming violent. Demons started manifesting and began talking. As I observed, I asked God what kind of demons were troubling this lady. The Spirit of God told me that the demonic forces that were on her were the demonic forces of night dancing and cannibalism.

Cannibalism is alive even today. Some of the people that are suffering from this kind of demonic possession go out to the graveyard where they use evil spirits to bring up the dead bodies. Then, they take them home and cook them.

As I confronted the evil spirits in this lady, they cried and begged. But after it all, she was totally and completely delivered. After she was delivered she told me her story. When she was six years of age, her parents took her to her grandma. This grandma was a night dancer. The girl was cut on her chest and back where the grandma then planted witchcraft in the body of that young girl. The grandmother put harbs in those wounds. She was told that she was being treated so that the evil spirits would stay away from her, but really, this grandma was planting the demonic possession right within her.

The young lady said that from that time, at six years old, she started going night dancing. Those evil spirits came to her in the middle of the night. She would just wake up. She wouldn't know what she was doing. She would open the door. If the key was hidden, she would find the key. She would run out in the night and find herself in the graveyards dancing and dancing.

Many times she would go with her grandma. When she would come to herself, she would be back in the home completely naked and she would find that they had a dead body. The grandma told her that they needed this body so that they could live, but that she was to never tell anyone about it, not the neighbors, no one. The grandma told her, "If you tell anyone about this it will be your time to die."

So, that young girl lived in fear. When she reached twenty-one she got married and the night dancing continued. She planted those harbs in the husband and he began night dancing also. However, there came a time when she felt that she was very tired of the terrible things she had done. She didn't want her children to be controlled by that demonic possession. That's why she had come to be born-again, that she might be free. She had heard from her friends that those Born-agains can help.

There is no situation that is impossible. She got born-again, as did her husband and the whole family. I encouraged her that Jesus had delivered her and healed her. I told her that she was now completely alright. I praised the Living God for what He did for that lady.

~*~*~

"In the biggest newspaper in our country of Uganda, the **New Vision**, on October 4, 2002, page seventeen, there was a very big story about a young man called Sseruwu. He is a resident of Mangira Village, Nakibano parish, Nagoje, Mukono District.

This young man was caught roasting the body of a child who had died and had been buried three days. Sseruwu had eaten some of the parts. Police tried to arrest him, but he ran away. People tried to chase after him, but they could not catch him because he was "running like the wind."

According to the newspaper article, three days later Sseruwu was found digging up another body four miles from his village. This time he was arrested and taken to the police station. A newspaper reporter visited him at the police station, and asked him, "Do you eat human bodies?"

"Yes," he answered, and he went on to say that it is not a crime to eat something that has been thrown away.

The newsman asked him what attracted him to dead bodies. Instead of giving a clear answer, Sseruwu asked,

"What attracts you to dead animals, like cows? Cows and other animals are edible, everyone knows that. When a person dies, he changes from human to something else. He or she is meat that should be eaten. It is not a crime." He then went on to defend himself.

The psychologist was quoted as saying that Sseruwu is mentally sick, but, as a minister of the Gospel, I know very well that this is demonic. I am bringing stories like this to let people know that if we are going to help people we have to admit that such demons are real and that they trouble people. It is the power of our Lord Jesus Christ that helps these people." - Pastor Kaweesa

~*~*~

HOLY SPIRIT WARNS WITCHDOCTOR

We went to Bukumula to conduct our first crusade almost five years ago. Many people came out for that crusade. As I was preaching, the Lord spoke to me that among the people attending the meeting there was a witchdoctor who had been a night dancer and a cannibal for a very long time. The Lord said that unless he became born-again, he was going to suffer a very terrible sickness where he would start to rot one part of the body after another.

This man was in the meeting. I spoke to him and pointed at him, but he did not repent. He ran away and did not come back to the crusade grounds. Some of our Christians went and gave him the Word of the Lord, but he refused to listen. After our crusade in that area a new church was born and many people who received Jesus as their Lord and Savior started to come to church.

During the next six months the witchdoctor continued with his night dancing and cannibalism. This man had bewitched the whole village and all the people of the village hated him and had nothing to do with him. They feared him.

The time came when he brought in a dead person and tried to eat it, but could not eat it. I don't know all the details. He fell very sick and started rotting one part after another. He was living by himself. No one had ever seen such a kind of sickness that could make a person rot one part at a time. Rot the leg, rot the arm, it was a terrible experience. He continued rotting one part after another until the time came when he finally died. He died a very, very terrible death.

That is what the devil does. He only comes to steal, kill and destroy. The devil killed him. Jesus loved him. The gospel message had come to his village, but he had refused to hear it. He didn't want the gospel. He wanted nothing to do with it. He had served the devil for a long time. The demonic forces repaid him with that kind of torment and suffering.

So, that man died like that. The people in the village refused to bury him; he was left in the house to rot.

The thief does not come except to
steal, to kill and to destroy.
I have come that they may have life,
and that they may have it more abundantly.
John 10:10

~ Ten ~

ALL IN A DAY'S WORK

And whatsoever ye shall ask in My name,
that I will do, that the Father may
be glorified in the Son.
If ye shall ask anything in
My name, I will do it.
John 14: 13 - 14

Steven Kaweesa

DELIVERANCE BRINGS PEACE

As I was on my bicycle heading back home the rain came. Not able to go any further I looked for temporary shelter. I came to a home where a woman invited me in out of the storm. Her name was Mrs. Mugerwa. Here in our country sometimes the rainstorms are so heavy that you cannot go anywhere, especially when you are on a bicycle like I was.

As I was there in Mrs. Mugerwa's home, I began sharing the Lord with her. I didn't know that she was having a very big problem. As I shared with her, the Lord began to reveal to me the problem that she was experiencing.

Every night when Mrs. Mugerwa went to bed she left her light on. The reason being, that evil spirits would come and torment her and try to kill her. She had suffered this for some years. I told her about Jesus who can save and redeem and cast away all those devils. She became born-again. The Lord then told me to tell her that she should bring all of her witchcraft to the church so it could be destroyed.

She brought a very big bag of witchcraft. There were many things in the bag. As we proceeded to burn and destroy everything there was a packet that began to jump and jump. Those evil forces are real. But, however real they may be, the power of God is more than enough. Mrs. Mugerwa was totally and completely set free. She came to the church and testified and we gave glory to God and thanked Him for saving her.

She told us that the Lord maybe loved her more than He loved us. She reasoned this because she had not been serving God, and yet, the Lord brought the heavy rains so that a minister of the Gospel could share with her about Jesus.

Mrs. Mugerwa started coming to church, and her family got born-again, her husband and their four children. She was very thankful to God.

~*~*~

ABUSED WIFE RESTORED

As we were going house to house preaching the gospel we came to a certain lady's house. We had not met her and did not know what difficulties she was going through. She had not told us. However, the Lord revealed to me, "That lady is very much abused by her husband. She is beaten time after time." Even her food was measured out to her in grams. If she took too much, she may be whipped.

(Many ladies here in our country are so abused through beatings. It is demonic. I hate it and am very concerned for these ladies.)

I told this particular lady what the Lord had showed me and she began to cry. As we ministered to her I told her that the Lord was even able to change the heart of the husband. She became born-again.

We had gone to her home at around eleven o'clock. That evening, before she could say anything to her husband, he said, "My wife, I am sorry. I have been abusing you, but from today on I will stop that abuse. And, I will stop measuring the food."

This lady could not believe what she was hearing. But, in her heart, she thought that if she told him she was born-again he would perhaps return to his former state. So, she kept quiet for some days until she could no longer contain it. She knew in her heart that it was Jesus who had done that powerful miracle in her life and home.

She finally told her husband, "I got born-again. On that very day when you came back and repented, that is the day that the pastors came and prayed for us." He was very amazed and said that he wanted to see the pastors. He, also, became born-again, as did the whole household.

God is so good. God is so wonderful. God is very, very much able.

~*~*~

THE HEALING OF HEARTS

The Redeemed Church in Kabowa invited me to minister in their seminar for three days, which I did. This is the church which I ministered in during the times of Idi Amin. Always, I feel honored when I am invited to minister there. I make sure that I am there when they invite me.

It was my second day of ministry and as I was getting on with the sermon, the Holy Spirit directed me to a certain lady in the service. I walked closer to her as I was going on with my preaching. The Lord told me to have a close look at her eyes, which I did. As I was looking into her eyes she started crying so loud. The Lord told me to tell her that after the service she should come to me and tell me what she did last week. So, she came to me.

135

I instructed her, "Please, tell me everything that you did last week. Don't hide anything." She began crying and crying. I laid my hands on her as I prayed in the Spirit, not audible. She was the ladies leader in her church. The pastor trusted her very much.

She said, "Pastor, I was deceived. I have been married for over ten years, but am barren and want children very badly. I have a friend who is not born-again." She then explained how her friend told her about a very, powerful witchdoctor that even the Born-agains visit and this witchdoctor helps them. The ungodly woman convinced this sister that the witchdoctor was not going to take away her God, but that she would receive medicine that would help her to have children and then she could go back to her church. So, she went to the witchdoctor who was from Tanzania.

Here in our country, it is believed that the witchdoctors who come from Tanzania are even more powerful than Ugandan witchdoctors. When a witchdoctor comes from Tanzania, he is held in high regard by the people who go to him.

When this lady went to the witchdoctor, she was given two kinds of "medicine", as they call it, but it is witchcraft. It is demonic. She was told to find a big graveyard when no one was watching. She was told to go a bit late in the dark and to start throwing that type of "medicine" to the north, the south, the east and the west. She was also instructed to call out to the demons to come and help her to be able to conceive, to call out to the spirits of the dead to rise up and give her children. The witch doctor warned her to not take that witchcraft into her house, saying that if she did, all her family would die.

Then, she was given another witchcraft that she was to take in to her house and hide it where no one would know where it was, not even the husband, only herself. She was told that if anyone else saw that "medicine", the whole house was going to die.

Can you see how people are deceived? How can you allow the devil to take advantage over your life? This sister was born-again and allowed herself to do all that. This particular sister was a leader in her church, and she had allowed herself to be deceived in such a manner as that.

I asked her, "What are you going to do about this? Do you know where you are going if you die?"

She answered, "I will go to hell. I know that I will go to hell. I know that God is angry with me. I have sinned and have had no peace since I did that. I am ready to repent."

I asked her, "How are you going to repent?"

She said, "I am repenting to God and to my husband. I am going to repent to my pastor and my church. And, I am repenting to you."

I said, "If it comes from your heart, that's the right thing to do."

She then asked me, "Pastor, help me. Can you come to our house so that I may repent to my husband? It may be that if I tell my husband, he may beat me and send me away from my house and seek a divorce." So, I made arrangements, that before I finished the revival meetings, to help her.

We went down to her home and she brought out everything. She repented before God and her husband. The husband cried. He said, "I have never demanded a child from my wife. I have always known that children come from God. I have always encouraged my wife to let us believe God and pray. I don't know how she was deceived."

The husband forgave his wife and said in front of us, "Dear, I love you. I know that God may help you give birth. And, even if you don't ever have children, I still love you." We prayed together for the healing of their hearts.

When we returned to the church, I told them that this sister had something to say. I told them to not be judgmental, but to sympathize with this sister.

She shared before them, "I am a sinner. I repent to my God, my pastor and the church. I had forsaken my faith and I was deceived." She explained the whole story. When she had done that the whole church went down on their knees. The power of the Lord came down in a mighty way. I didn't even preach. The Holy Spirit began directing me to people who had been hiding things in their homes, places of work, and in their hearts. Everyone was repenting. After that, a spirit of joy came and we experienced the joy of the Lord!

~*~*~

NOTHING HIDDEN

A certain woman, called Grace, came to me for counseling. I had never seen her before. After I had greeted her, the Lord told me to ask her if she was born-again. She told me she was. The Spirit of the Lord then told me to ask her the same question a second time, which I did. Grace again answered, "Yes." The Lord told me to ask her a third time, which I did, and she answered emphatically, "Yes!"

After that, I asked her, "How long have you been born again?"

Grace answered, "Six years."

Then the Lord spoke to me to ask her, "If you are born again, why do you drink liquor?" The Lord had showed me that under her bed was a big bottle of liquor and a glass.

I asked her, "Sister, if you are born again, what is that bottle of liquor and glass doing under your bed?"

Grace could not answer that. She was very much afraid. The Spirit of the Lord also went on to show me a very big bag of witchcraft. The bag was green in color.

The Lord told me to ask her, "If you are born again, what is that bag of witchcraft doing in your bedroom?" She could not answer. I said, "Lady, you have been deceiving yourself for the last six years that you are born again. I want to let you know that God loves you and He wants to help you. Today, I am not going to pray for you, but you go back and bring to me that witchcraft tomorrow. We will burn the witchcraft. And, as of today, you stop drinking that liquor."

The next day she came back with a very large green bag full of much witchcraft. Some things I had never seen before. We destroyed it all. I then shared with her about the love of Jesus, the Jesus that forgives sin and can save. I prayed with her and she became a true Born-again. She was very happy from that time on.

The Lord is so good. He can reveal any thing, any matter.

~*~*~

KARAMAJONG COME TO THE LORD

In our ministry we have gone to very many places to conduct crusades and seminars. In villages and cities we work with our churches. Where we don't have a church we work with friendly churches. No matter how difficult the place may be we go. The most important thing is that if the place we are going to has no church, then before we go, we make sure that we are able to plant a church there. We don't go to a place which has no church and then not plant a church there.

We have seen God in our crusades. Thousands have come to Christ. One time, a young man from Karamoja got born-again. Karamoja is one of the most difficult and backward places in our country. The Karamajong are warriors and they are cattle keepers. Their main food is blood and milk, all uncooked.

The Karamajong have a belief that all the cattle in the whole world belong to them, and if anyone else has any cattle it is because they stole them from the Karamajong tribe. So, time and time again they invade nearby tribes, like the Atesos and the Langis, and steal away their cattle. Not only that, but they make sure they kill everyone that they can find.

So, when this young man got born-again through the ministry of Eddy, one of our missionaries, all of us were very happy. He asked us if we would go and visit his home area and minister to the people there. All of us knew that we had desired to go to Karamoja, but we didn't see the door open. We thought that maybe this was the door for us. And, if we could put this young man in our Bible College, then the work could start there.

But, for me, as a person, I had some fear because I had heard that in Karamoja, every man, young and old, has a gun. When Eddy asked me if I would go, I said yes, trusting that the Lord would keep us safe. The day came and we went. There were three of us, Pastor Eddy, the young man, and I. We took our own food.

When we arrived, the first thing that amazed me were the many guns! Every man, young and old, was carrying a gun. Secondly, was that the men did not care about wearing clothes so much. The ladies were fairly dressed. Then, another shocking thing was the children, how they ate, how they had no clothes, and where they slept. It made me cry.

It was a rainy day and on that day, I knew that I was in a place that needed God. After the rain, the men started bathing in the dirty waters in the road and along the side of the road. I had never seen that before in my life. I had always thought that I had gone to difficult places, but this was difficult. As I observed all that, I began to wonder where we were going to sleep.

We were taken to a very big house in the midst of the bush. It was all in ruins. Some old cars were in the yard. As we were being taken to our bedroom we passed through the living room. It was no longer a living room, as cows and goats slept in there. Our bedroom had not been cleaned since the father died, which was nine years ago. We learned that this young man's father had been a government minister during the '80s and had since died.

"My brother and sister, in the midst of all this, we encouraged ourselves to preach the Word. What I have learned is that sometimes men and women of God tend to think that they have done much. But, when you go to such places and people it shows you how small we have done. And, how big we still have to do!

There are many places all over the world where people have never heard the Gospel and it's up to you and me to reach these places. Going to Karamoja was an eye opener that a lot of places need us." - Pastor Kaweesa

The young man left us in our bedroom and he then went out and invited people to come and hear the Gospel. The houses were far from each other and it took a lot of time to reach every home in an area like that. However, the word went out like wildfire and that evening over two hundred, with over a hundred children, came. Men came with their guns.

Eddy preached that night and when we gave the call for those who had received Jesus, every hand went up. Eddy wanted me to pray for them, but within my heart I was wondering whether they understood well what Eddy had said, or maybe the interpreter had said his own words. I asked again for those who had received Christ to raise their hands, and every hand went up. I have been a preacher for almost twenty-seven years, but I don't remember a meeting or crusade where all the people got born-again. It was one of the greatest miracles I had ever seen! We cried as we saw the love of Jesus on the Karamajong.

We had always heard that this area was bad news, but now the Good News of Jesus had come into their lives! We prayed with them as they received the Lord. We also prayed for the sick and the Lord healed them. Then, we went ahead and showed them the Jesus film. This made them even happier and they went away glorifying the Lord that night. The house we were staying in was not good, but, I tell you, we slept very good that night.

The next morning we went for a tour of their homes. We heard the testimonies of how many had received Jesus at the meeting. That second day more came to the Lord, and on the third day, over three hundred were born-again! When we told them that we would be leaving to go home the next day, they cried. We also cried. We wondered what we were going to do, because we didn't have a plan to start a church so soon. But, we left on the fourth day full of joy.

One month after our visit to Karamoja we went to check on the work there. We didn't know what to expect because there was no pastor or Bible there. We found that the Christians in Karamoja were still strong! And to our amazement, about sixty of them were meeting every day to have a time for God's Word and prayer. They didn't have a Bible. They were using the words that they had heard from us. No one had written our words down and I didn't know if there was someone who knew how to read and write. They were also evangelizing, praying for the sick and casting out demons! It was amazing!

We have sent groups a number of times to Karamoja. It is our prayer that the Lord will give us men from that area whom we can train and send back. Karamoja is a land of hope.

~*~*~

A LADY WITH A SNAKE?

It was on a Sunday morning as I finished preaching, when the Spirit of the Lord spoke to me that there was a lady in the congregation that had a snake. In my heart, I said, "Lord, a lady has a snake? Can a lady keep a snake?" The Lord confirmed to me that it was true. I didn't ask what kind of snake or how the snake came.

Two ladies came forward for prayer and we laid hands on them and prayed for them. The Lord showed me that one of the two ladies was the one with the snake, but He didn't show me which lady. After praying I sent them back to their seats and we continued praying for all the other kinds of sicknesses. I didn't tell the lady with the snake to come back and talk to me. I knew that the Lord had taken away that situation whatever it had been.

"Friend, sometimes when the Lord tells me something for the people in the service I call that very person to come forward, knowing who that person is. Other times, the Holy Spirit may tell me the problem and not which particular person. Sometimes, when you call out the problem, a number of people may come up for prayer. In that case, what I do is pray for each one trusting the good Lord to help out that very person the Lord told me about. That works." - Pastor Kaweesa

After one week, that lady, named Margaret, came to my office and explained her situation. For eight years she had suffered a terrible experience. Every night when she went to bed to sleep, a very big snake came and started crawling on her body. She tried to fight it. She knew that that situation could not be treated medically, so she went to the witchdoctors.

As I have told you, that's what the people do here in Africa, the ones who do not know Christ. When they get those kinds of troubles and situations, they will go to a witchdoctor to try to get help. So, that is what Margaret did, but there was no help for her. Going to the witchdoctors only adds to the problem, because the devil comes to steal, kill and destroy.

One night as Margaret saw that this situation was happening, she brought all four of her children to bed with her. She didn't tell the children what she was suffering from. And it was amazing, the children didn't feel anything. The children didn't feel the snake, only Margaret did. So, she had kept the situation to herself. She did not even tell her close friend, only the witchdoctor where she went.

However, after we prayed that morning at church, she said that the snake never came back to her. That demonic force in the form of a snake disappeared completely and Margaret was totally and completely delivered. She gave glory to the Almighty God!

~*~*~

LYDIA'S TANGLED WEB

There was a person in our church who was behaving like a girl. Most everyone thought this person was a girl, she even joined the choir. She was called Lydia. This person put on dresses and all kinds of make-up as ladies do. She was one of the most active young girls we had in our church.

However, some people watched her and the way she looked and they didn't think she seemed to be a girl and they began accusing her, "You are not a girl. You are a man." We, as pastors, took time to pray about Lydia's situation, but we didn't seem to get the answer from God.

A number of times when we went to our crusades the young girls would go to get their water in a group and they would start bathing. These girls would call out to Lydia, "Come with us and we will go bathe. Why don't you take off your clothes, Lydia?" She would decline and she would just stand there and watch the girls bathing.

So, when the time to sleep would come these young girls would say, "Lydia, you refused to bathe with us; you are not going to sleep with us!" Then, the old mamas would say, "Okay, our girl, you come this way." So, Lydia would just cross over and go to the mama's side.

Although the murmuring about Lydia continued, some years passed by. Then, one day, I felt that I could not take it any longer so I called Lydia to my office along with three other ladies from our church. I had the other ladies join us so that Lydia would not be able to come up with a bad story about me.

I said, "Lydia, can you talk to me please? This is confidential. We want to help you. I have been hearing this rumor for quite a long time. They tell us you are a man. Can you please tell us, are you a man?"

Lydia completely denied it. She then gave us various excuses how she had been fighting a beard and had been taken to doctors and the medication they had given her had not helped. She was shedding tears. Her voice was completely that of a woman. I talked to her at great length, as did the other ladies who were there.

Finally, Lydia announced, "As for me, I am a woman. You have known me all this time since I was born-again."

I then remembered a testimony that Lydia had shared with us about an incident that had happened before she was born again. How God had loved her and watched over her even then. She and a group of girlfriends were coming home from a nightclub, when some men came and ambushed them and raped all the women, except Lydia. As she had testified of that the whole church clapped and praised God for how He had protected her. We thought, "What a wonderful miracle!" And, yet, we were deceived.

We continued to talk to Lydia and tried to help her, but she continued to tell us, "I am a woman."

Finally, I told her, "Lydia, if you are deceiving us even today, you are deceiving us the last time. I am going to pray and within a few months time you are going to land into the hands of the security men. You are going to be discovered and when you are it is going to be terrible for you because you will go to prison. You will suffer a long, long time because this is against nature, against God's will, and against the law which governs this country. So, you are going to be in trouble. However, if you will say the truth today we will help you. And the incident, of which I have told you about, will not happen to you. I want to ask you this one thing. I have never asked it of anyone before, and I don't think I will ever ask it of anyone again unless he misbehaves in the way we are suspecting you. Will you allow me to ask this of you?"

She answered, "Oh, yes, Pastor. Go ahead, Pastor. You know I love you, Pastor. Every time you call me, I come, Pastor. What you tell me to do, I do. Have you ever told me to do something and I refused?"

I said, "No. You are very obedient. You go to the crusade. You are very involved in the church. For that, we are thankful."

I continued, "Now Lydia, I am going to leave this room. These are your fellow ladies. Do you fear them?"

She answered, "No, I do not fear them. I know them."

So, I said, "Okay. I am going out of the room and I want you to undress and show these ladies your nature so that they may confirm that you are really a girl. If that is confirmed, then I am going to stand up in the pulpit Sunday and publicly tell those that have been spreading rumors to stop. I will tell them that Lydia is a woman and not a man as some of them have been suspecting." I asked her, "Is that okay with you?"

She said, "Oh, yes, Pastor. That's okay, Pastor."

I said, "Okay, ladies, let me go out and you go ahead." So, I went outside and closed the door. I sat down and waited to see what was going to happen.

The first lady, Mrs. Mubiru, came out and when I asked her why, she answered, "Lydia said that I may not be a good lady, that maybe I am one of the ladies taking rumors around. She told me to go out." So, she came out.

Then, a few minutes later, the second lady, Sister Susan, came out. (Remember, I had three ladies, plus Lydia. Now, the second lady came out.) Lydia had told her that she suspected that she also was not right. So, now we only have one lady left in there with Lydia.

As Lydia was trying to undress she turned to this last sister and said, "Sister, you know we are ladies. I am in my monthly period. I did not come prepared for this. Please, I know that I am a woman, but are you okay if I take off my tops only?"

By now this third lady was trembling and wondering, "Oh, my God, this may be a man and he may rape me." So, when Lydia said that, this sister said, "Okay, okay. You just stop and don't worry. Do not worry. I understand." And she left Lydia in the office to dress.

When I heard that I knew that Lydia was trying to deceive us. However, I had prayed and I had warned Lydia. So, I told the ladies, "You wait and you will see what is going to happen in a few months. God is going to bring him or her out completely." And, that is exactly what happened.

Months went by. Even another pastor tried to help her, but she refused. Eventually she left our church and went to another small church. When she went to that church, they made her to be the head of the women's department. She sat with their women, gave them advice, talked to them, and encouraged them. And they loved her so much. They thought, "This is a great lady!"

We have a custom here in our country. When a young woman is going to introduce the young man that she is going to marry to her parents, she takes a large company to go along. They are all dressed beautifully in traditional dresses for such an occasion. It's wonderful; it looks beautiful. Lydia was very active in helping with that. She had been a matron in a number of weddings. She was always right there on the frontline. But, still some of us doubted her.

Well, it happened, as I had warned Lydia, that she landed in the hands of the security policemen. As she was there, the policewoman was talking to her and trying to get information. As she looked very closely, the policewoman said, "No, this must be a man. We have to check on you." Lydia then tried to fight the policewoman. The policewoman called for reinforcements which came and helped her. They got a hold of Lydia, undressed her, and found that she was a man! They shouted, "This is a man!" Oh my, when they discover that, it is big trouble in our country.

They put Lydia in prison. He was tried, found guilty, and went to prison for a full, complete year.

Now, Lydia is out of prison. He came back to our church and repented. He confessed he was deceiving people. He was very, very sorry. He had done that for ten good years.

Now, he is a man. He is happy. We forgave him and he is living quietly.

"My Friend, today there is a lot of deceit going on. There are people who call themselves born-again, and yet they are not. Maybe you are living with sin in your life. Please, it is high time you repent and turn to God totally. Don't allow that spirit of deception to go on in your life." - Pastor Kaweesa

~*~*~

QUESTION & ANSWER

Q: Pastor Stephen, from your own ministry experience, do demons exist? And, if they exist, can they possess people?

A: Yes, definitely. Sure, there is no doubt about it. We know that the devil is in this world. That he was cast away from heaven. In the ministry of Jesus Christ, time after time, when we read the Gospel of Matthew, when we read the Gospel of Mark, when we read the Gospel of Luke, when we read the Gospel of John, when we read the Acts of the Apostles, we find that in all different places, they met people that were possessed of demons. And, they cast out demons.

In Matthew 4:23, it says, "Jesus went throughout Galilee, teaching in their synagogues, preaching the good news of the kingdom, and healing every disease and sickness among the people."

151

So, demons exist. They are there. I have encountered them. I have prayed for people who have been suffering of demonic possession.

Ye are of God, little children,
and have overcome them;
because greater is He that is in you,
than He that is in the world."
1 John 4:4

~ *Eleven* ~

DEVIL CASTING

*I have strength for all things in Christ
Who empowers me – I am ready for anything
and equal to anything through Him Who infuses
inner strength into me, [that is, I am
self-sufficient in Christ's sufficiency.]
Philippians 4:13 AMP.*

"Friend, please allow me to share with you some experiences I have had in the demonic possession. I believe that the Bible does not specify that casting out devils is a special ministry gift. However, I have discovered that there are some ministers that are very gifted in demonic casting.

The Lord has given me this ministry during all these years. I have gone to places where the Lord has given me discernment and as I looked people in their faces, I could discern that one has a demon. And, sometimes as I discerned that, the demons would manifest.

The following kinds of examples show us that God is so wonderful, so powerful, and so glorious. This kind of devil casting is done here not only by me, but by other ministers. Demonic forces are real. But, the good thing is is that Jesus cast them out." - Pastor Kaweesa

DEMON SPEAKS TO ME

One year after I was born again I became a pastor and started in the ministry. There was a great need for pastors. The Lord had given me His Word, and also the gift of healing. Ministry gifts were manifesting in my ministry. Church elders recognized that the Lord was using me, so I soon found myself pastoring a congregation. This was during the terrible times of Idi Amin.

We had a small place for an office, which also worked as a prayer room. I had decided to pray and fast for three days and three nights. It was a total fast, I was not eating or drinking. As I was doing this, on the third day, a very tall, big lady came to my office. I was very weak and I did not want to be bothered, but she had come and I knew that I had to help her.

I asked her, "What is your problem?" Instead of answering me she stood right up there at the door and opened her eyes very, very wide. I had never seen someone opening wide the eyes like I saw that lady doing. She opened her eyes very, very wide and pointed her finger. Whether this was in a vision, or it was in the real sense, I cannot tell. But, I saw her fingers narrowing and becoming long.

As her fingers were coming towards me a very terrible voice came out of her, saying strangely, "You, young boy, I am going to kill you today! Who brought you here? Who told you to do this? You are going to die."

I was a bit scared because that was my first time to see something like that. Remembering how I had seen ministers stretch out their arms to those who are having demons, I stretched out my arm towards this lady, pointed one finger, and commanded, "You demonic forces, in Jesus' name, I charge you to come out of this lady!" When I spoke that, those demons got hold of that lady and brought her down on the floor. She fell down very hard.

The demons started screaming and crying and begging, "Please, please can you leave us? Let us go. Let us go."

I felt strengthened and charged them, "Leave her and be gone right now in the name of Jesus." The demons left her and she was totally and completely delivered. This lady was not born-again. Someone had directed her to come to our place. I shared with her Jesus Christ and she became born-again.

She told me how she had suffered that kind of demonic possession for twelve years. She explained to me how it had come about. There was a certain gentleman whom she refused to marry. He told her, "You will never get married and you will never have peace until you marry me." From that time on this lady started getting all kinds of trouble and pain. She could feel movements from her legs up to her head. And these things would move and move. She was living in terrible pain.

The movements and pain left at the same time I prayed with her and she was delivered from her demonic possession. No matter how strong the demons are Jesus has defeated every demon.

And these signs will follow those who believe:
In My name they will cast out demons....
Mark 16:17

~*~*~

YOUNG BOY SUSPENDED IN MID-AIR

One morning I was awakened at three o'clock by a woman screaming right at my door. She shouted, "Please, Pastor, come and help us! Come and help us!"

I asked her, "What is the problem? Are there thieves?"

She only said, "Please come and see, come and see." She could not tell me the exact problem which was taking place. I dressed and said a few prayers.

This lady was a Catholic. We had shared with her about Jesus Christ, but she had refused totally. She didn't even want to see us in her home. Now, here she was at my house crying and seeking help. So, I went with my Bible.

We hurried to her house and before they opened up the door I could hear voices scream, "Don't kill him! Don't kill him!" I opened the door. Children were crying, "Don't kill him!"

The lady pointed, "See?" When I looked into the living room, there was a twelve-year old boy just floating in the air. He was not hanging on to anything, not a tree, nothing at all. He was floating. This showed me that those demonic forces actually had power. I was a bit afraid because I had never seen that kind of experience, but instantly I knew that He who is in me is greater than who that is in that boy.

I pointed my finger to the boy and demanded, "In Jesus' name, you demonic power, you don't have power to kill that boy! Jesus died for that boy. I command you now, let that boy come down. And, you demons, make sure he does not get hurt!"

Slowly, by slowly, the boy began to descend. When he reached the floor, I grabbed him. The demons started screaming and begging, "Please leave us! Please leave us! We are sent, we are sent. We didn't mean to harm."

I rebuked the demonic forces, "I don't want to hear anything more from you! I want to see that you are gone in Jesus' name and let this boy be free." The boy was totally and completely freed and healed.

I went back to my house. It was now about 4:30 AM. I was very glad and thankful that the boy was delivered from that violent demonic possession. The next Sunday the mother of the boy, along with all of her five children, came to the church and gave their lives to the Lord.

~*~*~

MUSLIM WOMAN DELIVERED FROM SPIRIT OF DEATH

One day as I was in my office a Muslim lady named Medina was brought to me along with a companion lady. The men carrying her in just put her down without any greeting and they left. I looked her. She was almost like a dead woman. There was no movement in her body except the shaking of her head. She was able to talk, so I asked her what had happened.

Medina explained how four nights ago she had had a dream in which she saw her dead grandma who had died many years ago. Medina had never even seen this grandmother, for by the time Medina had been born, her grandmother was dead. But, it happened that this grandmother came to her in a dream.

In this dream the grandma was riding in a type of chariot that was used back in the days of the Roman Empire. The chariot was burning with fire. The grandmother was shouting to Medina, "I have come to take you! I have come to take you!"

Medina refused, saying, "No, no, no! You are dead! You cannot take me." The grandma was pulling her, but she refused to go. She woke up just as she was struggling and when she awoke she could not move at all.

The family was all Muslims. They waited until the second day and then they wanted to take her to a witchdoctor. But, Medina said, "No. I don't want you to take me to the witchdoctor. Take me to those people that I know pray for people and the people are delivered. You take me there. And, if I don't get healed I would rather die in the hands of God, than to die in the hands of the witchdoctor." So, she convinced her brothers and they brought her to me at the church.

When I heard all that I knew that the situation was serious. I knew that there was a spirit of death on Medina and that she needed deliverance. I opened my Bible and shared with her how Jesus came, and how God so loved the world that He sent His Son to save the world. I explained to her that it is only in Jesus' name that people can be delivered and saved. I told her that in her kind of situation Mohammed could do nothing to help, that only through Christ she could be set free.

I encouraged Medina first to accept Jesus as her Lord and then we would pray. So, she and the other lady both accepted the Lord. Then, I said, "I am going to cast those evil spirits out now." At that moment, the evil spirits took hold of her. She stood up and started screaming and then fell back down.

I got hold of her and said, "You evil spirit, you are not going to kill this woman! You do not have the power. If you were going to kill her, you would have had to do it before she reached here. Remember that Jesus died on the cross and bought her with a price. The blood of Jesus purchased this lady. So now, you demonic foul spirit of death, I rebuke you in Jesus' name. Be gone and leave this woman alone!" Instantly, Medina cried out at the top of her voice. The evil spirits started begging and crying. They said, "Why, Jesus, are you persecuting us? We wanted to kill this woman."

But, the evil spirits left, and Medina was delivered. I told her to stand up. She was totally and completely delivered.The woman who came with her was so amazed, she said, "I have never seen anything like this. In our region, we have never seen such a thing as this. From today, I really got born-again. I have accepted that Jesus. I want that Jesus to help me also and to empower me with His power."

So, we prayed that God would put more power in them. They left very happy. That was on a Friday. They came back to church on Sunday, bringing five ladies with them. Those five ladies also got born again. We gave the glory to the Almighty God!

"Remember, that this was a Muslim lady, coming from a Muslim family. The Lord loves the Muslims. Many times I have seen Muslims get saved.

From that time and on, in my ministry, I have been casting out demonic spirits. In some situations, the Lord tells me to cast out a spirit of death. And as I do that, time and time again, I have seen people get delivered from that terrible spirit.

What is amazing is that many of the people who have been delivered from that spirit of death will afterwards begin to tell me that they had been having dreams. In these dreams they would see themselves walking in a graveyard, or talking to people that had died long ago. Sometimes they saw people who had died calling to them.

However, time and time again, as I have prayed for these people, the Lord has delivered them out of that. And when they get this deliverance, such dreams stop coming.

And then, some people never have bad dreams and don't seem to have any problem and yet the Lord tells me to pray for a certain person because a spirit of death is coming against them. In that instance, I have seen the Lord deliver those people from accidents.

I remember one Sunday as I was ministering, the Lord told me to call out our brother, James. The Lord told me that the spirit of death was trying to kill him, and that we should break that. We prayed for this brother. The next day as he was traveling from Kampala to Kigali, Rwanda, the car he was traveling in got into an accident. There were three people in the car. The other two died, and only James survived." - Pastor Kaweesa

~*~*~

YOUNG MAN CONTORTS

A young man was brought to me who had suffered demonic possession for a long time. The demonic possession made this young man fold his arms and legs and become like a basket. That kind of situation had taken him for over five years.

As I have told you, the people here in Africa go to the witchdoctors for help. There is demonic power behind those kinds of sufferings and situations. People go to the witchdoctors to be freed and it turns out to be the same agents. They give their money and property, but they continue to suffer. This young man had been taken to a number of witchdoctors, but in vain.

So, we prayed for him, and as we did a voice cried out saying, "Why are you persecuting us? Why are you persecuting us? Everywhere we try to go, you persecute us. Why don't you leave us alone?"

I did not allow those devils to continue to confess all that kind of rubbish. In the name of Jesus, I rebuked them. This young man was completely and totally set free.

***

MADMAN ON CHURCH ROOF

There was a madman that ran and climbed right up on the roof of the church. He was moving up and down, up and down, up and down. He was shouting at the top of his voice. The whole village came. One strange thing here is that people are very quick to run and see what is taking place. You don't need to call. People just flock and come right there. So, that is what happened.

When the parents of this young man saw what was happening they went to look for the witchdoctor. Someone also called Pastor Robert. He came and looked at the young man who was right at the top of the church. About seventy people were there watching and saying, "Okay, let us see. They deceive us that Jesus heals, that Jesus casts out devils. Let's see now. This man is right on their church. Let us see what they are going to do."

When Pastor Robert came, holding his Bible, he looked at the man. He then stretched out his right hand to the man and commanded, "You, young man, in the name of Jesus, I command you to come down. And I command you to come down right now."

The young man crawled down instantly, saying, "I am coming." He came right down. The whole village was very amazed. Some people ran away, but some stayed. Then, Pastor Robert and his group of the Born-agains took this young man inside the church and prayed a prayer of deliverance. The young man stayed there that night and they prayed again the next day. They prayed the next day, also, and on the third day, that young man was totally and completely delivered.

~*~*~

BOY SEES WILD ANIMALS

There was a man who had a son that could see visions of all kinds of creatures on the wall moving, and creatures crawling on the floor. The boy would shout, "They are taking me! They are killing me! Help me! Save me!" He would cry and cry.

The parents tried as other people tried, going to witchdoctors. But, the situation was not getting any better, and this boy had now suffered for about three years. Eventually, the boy was brought to me.

When they brought him, he was crying and screaming, "I see a leopard! I see a lion!" He was seeing all kinds of animals. And, sitting in one place, he was trying to run.

We got a hold of him and I told him, "You are here now. Be calm. Even if you are seeing those kinds of creatures, this is the end. This is the last time for you to see those kinds of creatures. You are going to be set free in the name of Jesus Christ."

*And if I cast out demons by Beelzebub,
by whom do your sons cast them out?
Therefore, they will be your judges.*

165

But if I cast out demons with the finger of God,
Surely the kingdom of God has come upon you.
Luke 10: 19 - 20

We prayed a prayer for deliverance. The boy screamed and screamed. He opened his mouth so wide; he opened his eyes so wide. He brought out his tongue, and my, I had never seen a long tongue like that. Almost the whole tongue came out. It seemed as if this boy was going to die, but I said, "In Jesus' name, there is no demon which can kill this boy. It is now the blood of Jesus in control. Jesus loves this boy very much. You boy, be free in the name of Jesus." As I prayed, the boy eventually was totally and completely freed, just as it happened in the Bible in Mark 1:21-28.

I shared the gospel with the man who had brought the boy to me. He became born again. Even the boy confessed to believing in the Lord. It was very amazing. As people are in these kinds of situations they come to the Lord. They are very open to God's work and they are ready to receive. They are ready to accept because they need help.

~*~*~

WITCHCRAFT PLANTED IN YARD

A husband and wife came to visit me at my office and explained that they had suffered demonic possession for a long, long time. They said that whenever they would go to their bedroom at night, they would close and lock the door. After they had gone to bed they would hear footsteps come right up to their bed and someone would then get into the bed and sleep right in the middle of them. Then, a very strange and terrible thing happened, in that, this someone started to sleep with the lady and the husband could hear what was going on.

They tried to fight this situation by going to the witchdoctors who gave them all kinds of witchcraft. The witchdoctors also took all of their money. All the money they got they gave up to the witchdoctor, but the situation did not move away. They were very disturbed with this for ten years. They were exhausted and confused. Finally, they realized that they could do nothing about this kind of situation and that the only solution was to come to God.

The wife told her husband, "I am going to get born-again." The husband did not refuse her. So, she came to church and got born-again. Next, they came to my office and told me the problem they were experiencing.

I shared with them, according to Matthew 4:23 and 24, how Jesus went around doing good and casting out devils and evil spirits. As I prayed with them for deliverance, the Spirit of the Lord showed me where the evil spirits were coming from to disturb them. The Lord showed me that there was a tree in their yard where certain witchcraft had been planted. I instructed the husband to go dig around the tree and remove the witchcraft.

As he was digging around that tree, he came across a very large jar of all kinds of witchcraft. This jar contained blood and certain things they could not understand. It was all destroyed, and from that day on the evil spirit never came back again. They were completely free. They were so thankful to God.

For we do not wrestle against flesh and blood,
but against principalities, against powers,
against the rulers of the darkness of this age,
against spiritual hosts of wickedness in the
heavenly places. Ephesians 6:12

~*~*~

"Demonic forces operate in a system. They have a network. They have big commanders, and they have privates. They are like our armies around the world. They operate that way. These forces, as far as I know, operate in a person's life as they see necessary." - Pastor Kaweesa

DEMONS MASQUERADE AS DEAD HUSBAND

One day a woman came to me and told me that she was a widow, her husband having died five years earlier. She told me that every night when she went to bed, that same husband would come to her and sleep right on her. She had hated that thing and had gone to the witchdoctor.

I shared with her about Jesus Christ. I told her of the story in Luke 8:26-33 where Jesus went across the lake and met a violent man that was full of devils living in tombs. I shared with her how as Jesus was casting out those demons they begged Jesus to allow them to go into the swine that were feeding nearby. As Jesus allowed them to do that, the pigs ran into the lake and all drowned. But, the man was totally and completely delivered.

This lady was very much amazed that just one man had enough devils to go into 2,000 pigs! When she heard that kind of story, she gained strength, and her fear disappeared. Her eyes were wide open. She asked me, "Can Jesus do that for me? Can He set me free?"

I answered her, "Of course." I went on to explain to her that the husband's parents were not born again. I told her that sometimes the parents in that kind of situation will seek a witchdoctor to bewitch so that the lady would not be able to marry again. That was indeed their intention. The Holy Spirit also revealed to me that the family had planted witchcraft that they had received from the witchdoctor right at the tomb of the man.

I prayed with her and cast out that demon in the name of Jesus and that demon left. I thank Jesus that she was totally and completely free and those demonic forces never came back. Everything was put right. She now loves the Lord and is very grateful to the Lord.

"Sometimes in our country when a man dies, the family members of that man who don't want to see the widow re-marry will go the witchdoctor and get some witchcraft to bewitch the widow so that she will never get married again. They take the witchcraft to the tomb of the dead husband and plant it there. Then, demons in the form of the dead husband begin to come to the widow and sleep with her every night. In this way, the widow will be tormented for the rest of her life.

I call those deceiving spirits, because that dead man had no power to come back and attack this lady. However, the devil is deceitful and a liar. Those deceiving spirits got a picture of the dead husband and came back to trouble this lady.

Many widows with this kind of problem have come to me for help. I am thankful to God as I have seen each one of them delivered. The blood of Jesus is powerful!" - Pastor Kaweesa

LADY RECEIVES PEACE

Another lady had a very terrible experience, also. Her half brother had died three years earlier, but had been coming to her every night and sleeping on her. This lady suffered greatly. She had gone to the witchdoctors without success, then eventually she came to me.

I could see how damaged she was, her feelings and psychologically. It was very disturbing to have, who she thought was, her dead brother come to her. I shared with her the love of Jesus and she accepted the Lord. We prayed with her and thanked Jesus. She was totally and completely freed. She praised and thanked God for what He did for her.

~*~*~

"As I told you before, I have had a number of ladies come to me who have suffered with that same situation, but never a man. I want to remind you that these people are dead. They are not able to come to the living people. It is demons that are deceiving people.

A number of women have come to me with that terrible, torturing experience from the demonic forces. But, glory to the Almighty God, Jesus has enough power! Jesus is on the throne! He performs miracles! Demonic forces run away in Jesus' name!" - Pastor Kaweesa

A GOOD REPORT

One Sunday morning at our church in Seguku in 1999 we asked for church members to give testimonies. A lady with two children stood up. I did not recognize her and thought that she was a new lady. She gave her testimony.

She said, "Pastor Steve, I don't believe you know me, but I know you very well. In 1982 when you were the pastor at the Redeemed Church I was in the second year of my Senior Secondary School. I became mad and began throwing stones at people. I even started undressing myself and running in the streets. I slept outside. My parents took me to seek help from many witchdoctors, but in vain. Then, after suffering with this for over one year, I was no longer able to continue with school.

A friend, who was born-again, went to my parents and asked them to allow her to take me to her pastor for prayer. My parents agreed. They hired a taxi and two other people brought me to you for prayer. When you prayed, something like a very heavy burden lifted away from my body. From that day, I was healed."

Come to Me, all you who labor and are heavy laden, and I will give you rest. Matthew 11:28

She went on to tell us that she went back home totally healed and saved, and one month later she was back in school. She finished her Secondary School and went on to finish Nursing College. She got married and had two children. She told us that she and her husband were serving the Lord. She said that she had wanted all these years to share her testimony how a man of God was used of the Lord to save her life.

~*~*~

"I was amazed to hear from this lady. I didn't think that I knew her, and yet she knew me very well and through me she got delivered and saved. I have come across a number of people who tell me how I have helped them come to the Lord, and also people I have prayed for whom got wonderful miracles. And, I don't know these people at all.

My Friend, we are only people and we are limited sometimes. I think the Lord allows us to be that way, because it's only the Lord who is worthy to be given all the glory." - Pastor Kaweesa

"SHE'S MINE!"

One evening a lady came all the way from the east side of our country, from the Kenya border. This lady came looking for me, but I was not around. She found

Pastor Robert and decided to wait for me. When I did not turn up and she was about to leave, Pastor Robert told her that if she needed prayer, he could help her. She agreed to that.

They went to the office and she began to explain what her problem was. She said that she was suffering from a demonic spirit in such a way that every man who had tried to marry her was killed in a car accident. Pastor Robert asked her to explain how those men were killed. Was someone killing them, or what?

She explained that this had been going on for the last seven years. During those seven years, six different men had wanted to marry her. But, when the time of Introduction had come, each one of those men had been killed in an automobile accident within two weeks time. (In our country, the time of Introduction is when the girl takes the young man that she wants to marry to her parents. It is a very big occasion.) All six of those young men had met their death in the same way, and at almost the same time after Introduction. By now, people all over her village knew that if you try to marry her, you will die.

Pastor Robert agreed that this was demonic, that the devil was fighting this girl so she couldn't get married. Pastor Robert gave her Christ and she was born-again. As he was praying for her, she began screaming, "This is my wife! No man should ever marry her! She was given to me when she was young."

Many people in the world do that kind of witchcraft by dedicating their children to devils when they are still young. Pastor Robert went on to cast that evil spirit away and it was gone. As he was praying, this lady said that she saw a very tall man come out of her, crying at the top of his voice, "You have chased me away, and I am gone!" She was free from then on.

I have prayed with a number of women who have gone through this kind of torment by evil spirits. The Lord is faithful. I have seen each one of them delivered.

~*~*~

HELP IN NO OTHER NAME

The devil tries to torment people in very many ways, because his work is to kill, destroy and steal. One Sunday morning a lady came to our church from Masaka, which is one hundred miles away. She had heard about us and she had heard the gospel many times, but had refused it as did her husband. She was a strong Catholic. She hated the Born-agains.

It came about that this lady lost three of her four children in a very disturbing manner all within one year's time. The first child fell in a ditch and was found dead. She was four years old. The second child was found dead in his bed, and the third child, a two year old daughter, died one evening in the living room.

Right after they had lost the first child they went to the witchdoctor who assured them that the person who had killed the child would also die in just a few days. They were given all kinds of witchcraft for defense. But, they found out that this witchcraft didn't work as they continued to lose their children. After the loss of the third child, this lady and her husband went to another witchdoctor whom her parents praised as being one of the most powerful in the country. When they went there, they took all kinds of things. The witchdoctors here mostly ask the people to bring goats, chickens, cows, and sometimes they ask for new clothes.

"My brother and sister, you must pray for Africa. Often times when people are disturbed with demonic forces they go to the witchdoctors instead of coming to Jesus." - Pastor Kaweesa

This particular witchdoctor did his things, then he said to the woman, "I can't do anything much for you, because I see that even you and your only child are going to die in a few days." Upon hearing that, this lady ran away from the shrine. They tried to chase her, but in vain. As she was running away, the words of salvation that she had heard many times from the Born-agains, and refused, came to her mind. The most powerful words which came to her were, "Jesus loves you."

She wondered which church of the Born-agains she should go to. She had heard about our church in Seguku. So, very early on that Sunday morning she made up her mind to come. It was a very far journey. She hired a taxi from deep in the village to take her to the highway where she found a taxi to Kampala. Then, from there she got yet another taxi to the church!

We were in the middle of the service when she came all the way from the back to the front seat. When I called for those who wanted to give their life to the Lord, she was the first one to the altar. She was crying as she gave her life to the Lord.

As we began to pray for people for deliverance, she was one of those we prayed for. God's power came down and the demons in her started screaming that they wanted to kill her. But, God is good all the time. We cast

175

those demons out in Jesus' name and the lady became free. She has a new life now and is happy with the Lord Jesus Christ.

~*~*~

WITCHDOCTORS GET BORN-AGAIN

One time in 1993 at our village of Seguku, we were conducting a one week crusade. Many people got born-again as they do at the other crusades we conduct monthly. We see people coming to the Lord in great numbers. As I am writing today, the church in Uganda is growing at a very high speed, in the villages and in the cities. Many places we go to stage a crusade, people come in the thousands. So, by the end of this particular crusade, many people had turned to God. Among those who received Christ was a witchdoctor, named Nakabugo.

Nakabugo had been at her home in the shrine giving witchcraft to the people who had come to her that day. She didn't come to the crusade grounds, but she heard the Gospel through the powerful speakers. Thank God for those speakers! Nakabugo got born-again right there at her shrine!

Right away she told the people who came to her, "Please, from today, I am no longer a witchdoctor. I am born-again. Please don't come back here for witchcraft." Fearing to come in the open, she then sent a note to us asking us to burn her shrine with all the witchcraft. We accepted that invitation with great joy! We made the arrangement for the next day.

We prayed for Nakabugo, her three daughters and four grandchildren, then burnt her shrine along with all the witchcraft. The whole village came out because when they hear of such a thing, they want to come and see for themselves. Those who were not born-again gave Nakabugo only a few days to live, supposing that because she burnt the witchcraft, the demons would kill her.

Well, it's now been nine years, and Nakabugo still loves the Lord as do her children and grandchildren. She is a powerful lady for God.

~*~

Barry and Ruth visited us in 2001 from the U.S.A. They became very interested in visiting people's homes, the born-agains and the not born-agains. One home they visited was that of a witchdoctor named Saul Lwase. He was a very well known all over Uganda. People would line up at his shrine.

So, Barry and Ruth went to visit him, and he welcomed them. They introduced themselves and why they had come. He was open to the Gospel and gave them time to share about Jesus. At last, he gave his life to the Lord!

Saul came to church on Sunday and gave his testimony of how he had become born-again, and then went home that afternoon and gathered all the witchcraft he had been using and put it in the shrine. He had a lot of witchcraft things. He had some workers around the shrine. They wondered what he was doing, because he chased away every person who came for treatment that afternoon, telling them that he was now born-again and was no longer in the business of witchcraft. At first, they thought he was joking.

177

After he had gathered all the witchcraft things and put them inside the shrine, he got a fire and burnt the shrine. People made the alarm shouting, "Saul has gone mad!" But, he said, "I am not mad. I have accepted Christ and I am now taking on this new life in Jesus."

It is now coming up to two years since he got born-again. He told us that before coming to Christ, he was suffering all kinds of pain and he had no where to turn for help. He told us that he was living in fear and he knew that it was only God that could help him, but he didn't know how to get to God.

He told us how one day the Born-agains had come to the village looking for ground where they could stage the crusade. They had come to his house and he had offered them his ground, but the next thing he heard was that the crusade was going on in the village. He said that he cried that whole night, wondering how he could ever get out from the demonic bondage.

Saul Lwase is now a happy man! He even changed his name from Saul to Paul like the Apostle Paul of the bible changed his name from Saul. He is faithful to the Lord.

~*~*~

"My brother, many witchdoctors out there are hurting, looking for help. It is you and I who have the truth to go out and help them. As I minister and do outreaches, I have seen more and more witchdoctors come to the Lord.

In fact, this year, in one of our biggest newspapers in Uganda, the "New Vision", there was an article about witchdoctors. The article stated that witchdoctors, at their annual conference, voiced out that their biggest enemy is now the Born-again churches. Why? The article said it is because as the Born-agains pray for people they get healed, they cast out devils and demons, they conduct crusades and change people. And, they do not stop there, they have changed many of the witchdoctors and they bring their secrets out in the open. The witchdoctors, at their conference, agreed to see to it that they would work hard to stop the Born-agains so that they could not go on like that.

One thing I know is that Jesus gave us power over all kinds of demons, according to Matthew 10:1. The kingdom of darkness is being shaken in Uganda and the world over." - Pastor Kaweesa

Question & Answer

Q: Pastor Kaweesa, have you ever experienced a born-again believer being possessed by demonic powers?

A: In my experience, I have seen not one, not two, not ten, but even more than one hundred Christians that have had terrible demonic possession. Most theologians agree that a true born-again believer cannot be "possessed", but rather he or she can be "oppressed". However, I have seen this kind of possession by demonic forces.

What is very disturbing is to see that these men and women have walked with Jesus very faithfully and they love God. I cannot really tell you why they stay in that kind of bondage. What I think may be the problem, is that these

people need help. Although they have become born-again, still they need help because they come from very terrible families; they are coming from very terrible experiences. So, although they have accepted Jesus and they love God, still they need help to come out of these terrible situations.

Here in Uganda, I have found that the families are "clans". Many families are deeply involved in witchcraft. When they hear that so and so is born-again, they consider that that one is now their enemy. So, they will try to send demonic forces to attack the born-again person.

The newly born-again person needs help because they are young in the Lord and they don't know everything yet. I share scriptures which gives them encouragement. Their faith is built up and they realize that they have the right to live in total freedom. We pray with them and they receive help. If they are helped, there is no way that a Christian can stay possessed with demonic forces.

Another thing is that sometimes the pastors themselves do not believe that there are demons. So, if someone who is under the ministry of that kind of pastor becomes born-again and has that kind of problem, I don't think that person will ever be free.

Some people live in fear of demonic powers and that fear opens the door for this demonic thing. For some, it is a family curse that brings these kinds of problems. Until this kind of person sits down and gets counseling from a man of God, he or she will never be free. As I read God's Word, I see time and again the deliverance ministry of our Lord. Read, Luke 9:37-43, and Mark 7:32-35.

Truly, truly, I say to you, he who believes in Me,
the works that I do, you shall do also;
and greater works than these shall you do;
because I go to the Father.
And whatever you ask in My name, that will I do,
that the Father may be glorified in the Son.
If you ask Me anything in My name, I will do it.
John 14:12-14

Steven Kaweesa

~ Twelve ~

HEALING MIRACLES

He sent His word and healed them,
and delivered them from their destructions.
Psalm 107:20

WOMAN HEALED OF CANCER

Every Saturday we had a time that we prayed for people. We invited them just for prayer. This was not a preaching time, only prayer for those that were sick.

One time a lady named Miriam was brought who was very sick. She was very smelly. I asked her what she was suffering from and she told me it was cancer. In our country, there was only one place during that time where they treated cancer. She had been taken there and completed all her therapy, but her situation was getting worse and worse. She was dying. The cancer was down in her private parts and she was feeling a lot of pain. She could not walk. She could not move. She was always on the bed.

So, Miriam was brought to us during this time of prayer. She was Muslim in faith. I shared with her about Jesus Christ. I explained to her why Jesus had come into the world, to save and heal those who were afflicted, those who were sick, and those who were tormented by any kind of disease, even cancer, inclusive.

After I shared with Miriam, we prayed a prayer of faith. And although at that moment she still could not move, I assured her, "You are totally and completely healed." The four men, who had brought her, took her back to her home.

It came to pass that during the night, while she slept, she saw a dream. In that dream, she saw a hand that was very white and very bright. The hand took a hold of her and said, "I am Jesus. I am the Savior. I am the Lord. I love you. And, from today, I have healed you of cancer."

When she woke up, she wondered what the meaning of her dream was. But, then, she discovered there was no longer any pain in her body. She stood up from her bed. She found that she could move. She jumped around! She danced around! The sickness was totally and completely healed.

In the morning, she came to the church and gave her testimony. We praised the Living God for what He had done for Miriam. The whole church was in jubilation, because nearly everyone had seen how she had been brought in on Saturday. Miriam was completely and totally delivered.

~*~*~

YOUNG BOY HEALED OF CANCER

A young boy named Peter was brought to us by his mother. Peter was about seven years of age and had skin cancer. He had wounds all over his body that were bleeding. He was in pain.

The mother was not born-again. She had gone to hospitals and tried all kinds of medication. And remember, as I told you before, those that are not born-again, when medical treatment fails, seek the witchdoctors. They go to the witchdoctors, because they think that maybe it is that kind of sickness that someone has bewitched them. So, they go and check with the witchdoctors to consult the spirits to see why that sickness is on them.

This mother and her son had gone from one witchdoctor to another, and they had spent almost all of their belongings. Much like the woman in the Bible who had spent all she had seeking to be healed, but never got any help.

Eventually, a friend who was born-again shared with the mother how Jesus was able to heal her son of that terrible sickness. So, they brought Peter to us. We shared about the love of Jesus and the woman became born-again, even Peter accepted Christ.

Peter was in terrible pain and was crying. I laid my hands upon him and prayed a prayer of faith believing that God was going to heal that skin cancer. After seven days, Peter came back to me and the wounds had started drying up. I continued to pray. By the second week, the wounds were continuing to dry. And, by the end of the month, the wounds that had covered the whole body were totally and completely dried out. New skin was coming!

Today, Peter is completely healed. I met his mother after seven years, and she told me that the skin cancer has never come back. Peter is now a grown man. I thanked and praised God.

~*~*~

"I am continuing with the healing ministry. I have seen a lot of healings. I am giving you these examples so that you will be encouraged.

Friend, whatever kind of sickness you are suffering from, there is room for you to be healed and delivered." - Pastor Kaweesa

BLEEDING ULCERS HEALED

About eleven of us from our church were invited to Kenya in 1994 to conduct a seminar. In that seminar, we prayed for the sick. There was a young man who became completely healed. When we invited those who had testimonies, this young man stood up and told us the wonderful miracle which had taken place in his life.

He said that he was not born-again. He had suffered with bleeding ulcers for over five years. When that bleeding started, he could not do anything. He could do no work, and he could not go to school.

One day, he heard a voice that said, "If you go to that church, you will be healed of your sickness." This young man believed the voice even though he was not born-again. God is very wonderful. God can even speak to those that are not born-again. This young man heard that voice, and he came to the church and sat down.

As the message was going on, he felt power in his body. He said that he felt like electricity was right in his body. And, in that process, he felt a confidence that he had been healed of his sickness and that he would never see it again. He was very thankful and he said, "I now believe in Jesus Christ."

We led him to the Lord Jesus Christ and he was completely saved. And he was totally and completely healed. Praise the Lord!

~*~*~

DISEASED EYES HEALED

There was a young girl who was dying from a disease in her eyes. She was about thirteen years of age. The mother had tried all she could to help by taking her daughter to hospitals and also to the witchdoctors. When they came to us the eyes were red and shedding tears constantly. She was in a great deal of pain and could not open her eyes.

I led the girl and her mother to the Lord. They both received the Lord as their personal Savior. Her mother was very, very happy. She got the happiness right away! They left and came back after a week. The girl's eyes had been totally and completely healed! The eyes had cleared up and were white, instead of red. The mother was very thankful. We praised and thanked God!

Now, it has been almost ten years and the girl has grown to become a lady. I met her mother in town and she told me that her daughter has not suffered any more eye disease even up to now.

What we discovered is that when the Lord heals, that healing lasts. It's there. God gives it to us freely.

~*~*~

TUMORS DISAPPEAR

A lady came to us who was suffering from tumors in her tummy. She had been told that she must be operated on, but she was very, very scared. She did not want to be operated on. She thought that if she was operated on, she was going to die, so she said no.

That's when a friend of hers told her about the love of Jesus. When she came to me I shared with her and she became born-again. We prayed with her and the Lord healed her instantly.

When she went back to the doctor, the tumors were no more to be found, not a trace! She was free from pain. She was totally and completely healed.

~*~*~

FROM A DISTANCE

One time as I was visiting the U.S., the Lord gave me a vision of a lady in our church. He showed me that she was suffering in her tummy. The Lord told me, "Write to that lady and let her know that she has two tumors in her tummy. Tell her to go to her doctor and they will remove those tumors and she will be fine." So, I wrote the letter, laid my hands upon it, prayed a prayer of faith, and then posted the letter.

When this lady got the letter, she read it and believed it. She didn't know why she had been suffering. She had already gone to the doctor and they had examined her and found nothing. They had scanned her, but could not find what was wrong with her. They had even given her all kinds of medication, but it had not helped.

So, after reading the letter, she went back to the doctor and said, "I know what I am suffering from. I have two tumors in my tummy." I had told her exactly where the tumors were, which she shared with the doctor. The doctor asked her how she knew, and she said, "The Lord told me through my pastor. I want you to check."

So, they did more exploring, and the tumors were discovered. They removed the tumors and the lady was very, very happy. The doctors were very much impressed how God could see all those types of things right inside people's tummies. So, that lady was totally and completely delivered.

~*~*~

"On my side, I don't have a problem to understand that. I know that God is our Creator. He created us. He knew us before we were conceived. God knows us and where we are going. He knows what is outside of us and He knows what is inside of us, because He is the One who made us. He knows everything." - Pastor Kaweesa

RAISED FROM DEATHBED

A lady who was in a coma was brought to us during our time of prayer. She was very, very sick and dying. Her cancer was in a very advanced stage. In fact, the cancer had taken up the biggest part of her being. She was brought to us in hopes that we may be some kind of help. We told them, "We have the help. We can pray in Jesus' name and we know that when we pray, people get healed." And, I believed that the Lord could heal that lady even though she was in that terrible kind of situation.

"My Friend, I want to tell you that in any situation, whether people are in their last stages of sickness, even if they are in a coma, it is our duty to believe Jesus Christ. Jesus even raised people from the dead. So, we cannot just give up on someone because they are almost dying." - Pastor Kaweesa

So, I laid my hands upon this lady and we prayed. She regained her consciousness and she began to talk. She told me how the sickness had come about. She had gone through chemotherapy, but there was no help at all. She had suffered over three years in that condition.

I assured her, "We have prayed for you in Jesus' name. Jesus is good. Jesus has healed your sickness." They took her home and brought her back after two weeks. She had literally come back to life! She was completely healed! She could walk.

I thank Jesus for that kind of healing. It is only Jesus who can heal in such a manner like that.

~*~*~

BLINDNESS HEALED

A Muslim woman came to us when she was suffering from blindness. I shared with her about the love of Christ and said to her, "Okay, I am going to pray with you and believe God for you." I prayed and believed.

Although nothing seemed to happen, I told her by faith, "In the morning, your eyes will be completely and totally restored to you."

In the morning, this lady was totally healed from blindness. My, she went around thanking God, and telling people! Many people knew her. She praised the Lord! She got born-again and she thanked God for what He had done for her.

~*~*~

CANCER HEALED

As I was visiting a certain church, a lady whom I had never met came and gave this testimony. Her name was Margaret. (I had ministered at this church about one year before.)

About a year ago, Margaret had come to church very, very sick. She was suffering from cancer and the doctors had told her that they could do nothing more to help her situation. The relatives she was living with had told her that there was no more help for her and that the best thing she could do was to go to the village. Here in Uganda, when a sick person decides to go to their village, it means that they are waiting to die. So, that was the case with Margaret, they wanted to take her to the village.

They told her, "We are taking you to the village. We cannot do anything more for you. We don't want you to be here, because if you die right here we have no money for transporting your dead body." Margaret refused. She was very much discouraged and confused.

She came to the church. While I was preaching in that service she said that she heard a voice say, "I have healed you of cancer."

She went home still feeling very sick, but told her relatives, "The Lord has healed me of cancer." In a few weeks' time, she was feeling better and went to the doctor. They checked her and there was not any trace of cancer. She was totally delivered. This was a year later when she gave me that testimony.

God heals even cancer. Cancer gets healed in Jesus' name!

~*~*~

"I want to talk a little bit about the AIDS disease. You have heard about the AIDS disease, and we are living in a situation where AIDS is a threat not only to Uganda, but to the entire world.

AIDS was discovered way back in the '70s in our country. In Uganda, the first name that they called AIDS was "Slim". People who suffered that kind of disease began slimming and slimming and slimming until their whole body was completely right on the bones. You could only see bones on that kind of a person. And, by the time they died, their bodies were completely and totally gone.

In our ministry, I have seen the healing of AIDS. I thank Jesus that there is no disease that is above His healing power." - Pastor Kaweesa

WOMAN HEALED OF AIDS

There was a lady who came to us from Masaka, which is about one hundred miles away. She brought her sixteen year old daughter who was suffering from demonic possession. This daughter had suffered since she was four years old.

With that kind of demonic possession, the daughter would cry like an animal. She could produce animal voices. They had gone to witchdoctors for help, because they knew that this kind of sickness could not be treated in hospitals. So, they had gone and consulted several witchdoctors, but received no help. A friend shared with the mother about Christ and our church. She had tried everything else, so she asked, "Why don't I try Jesus?"

The husband had died nine years earlier leaving the mother with AIDS. She was going for treatment all the time. Although she was still looking healthy and strong, she knew she was living with that disease. When she came to us, she came for prayer for her daughter. She had given up on her own sickness; she was only waiting for the day she would die.

With those kinds of people, the first thing I do is share Jesus. They accepted the Lord. When we prayed for the daughter the demons manifested, but then ran away and she was totally and completely delivered.

After doing that, I wanted to know more about the mother. I told her that Jesus can even heal AIDS. I then prayed for her and commanded every virus to be killed in Jesus' name.

This lady took that very serious. She went back to the hospital and told them, "Do you know what? The Lord healed me of AIDS. The viruses have been completely and totally killed in my body, so there is no AIDS. I want to take a test." They took blood from her, tested it, and it was negative. She was very, very, very excited!

She came back to my place. Remember, she lives almost one hundred miles away, and here in Uganda to live one hundred miles away is a very, very long journey. You have to take taxis here and there. However, she came back and gave me her testimony, and we thanked God. We were so grateful for what the Lord had done for this lady.

But, it did not stop there! She told two of her friends who also had AIDS. In fact, one of them was in the advanced stages and was close to dying. She was living in constant pain. Both of those women came. I shared the love of Jesus Christ with them and then prayed for them. They went and took a blood test. Their blood tests turned out to be negative!

Jesus can heal AIDS. AIDS gets healed in Jesus' name!

~*~*~

DID THE MACHINES LIE?

A woman came to me crying and crying. She was not born-again at that time. She said, "Pastor, I want you to help me. My husband has several women. What can I do? I know already that I have AIDS and I don't want to die now."

I shared the love of Jesus with her, and then gave her my advice, "I am going to pray for you. I believe Jesus heals AIDS. After we pray, go for your blood test. If it is negative, come back here. If it is still positive, come back here and tell me." I continued, "You have to make a decision. Stay with your husband, and you will both die of AIDS. Or, go away from your husband, and stay by yourself. Know that we have prayed for you, and know that the Lord is healing you from AIDS. But, stay by yourself and help your children to grow with you."

This lady accepted that. She said, "Pastor, if I am totally and completely delivered from AIDS, I am going to live by myself." So, we prayed and she went for the blood test, which turned out negative. She was very excited!

She went back home and the next day she told her husband, "Husband, from now on I am not going to live with you. I don't want to die of AIDS. We have children. I have to help my children. I don't believe I have to die now. I was prayed for and I was totally and completely healed from AIDS."

The husband was very, very mad. He said, "Do you think you can stay by yourself and help all those kids? Do you have your money?" In Uganda, it is the man who chases the woman away. If she is misbehaving, he will tell her to pack up all her belongings and go away with her children. Many ladies here in Uganda are suffering in that kind of mistreatment by their husbands. Many of them are helpless to get a job. Oftentimes, these ladies have only been a housewife and it is very, very hard to get a job. However, that man left his wife in the house and he went and stayed with his other women.

One year later, he came back dying, in very deep pain. He came back and said to his wife, "Please forgive me. I was in the wrong. I am now dying of AIDS. May God help you to raise our children." She shared with him about Jesus, but he didn't take it seriously.

This lady was now very scared knowing that her husband was dying of AIDS. She didn't sleep that night. She wondered if those machines had lied to her. She was a bit confused. In the morning she ran to the hospital for another blood test. She was completely negative. The man died three weeks later. It has now been over five years and this woman is living happily with her children. She is very thankful to God. God has done a number of miracles in her life.

AIDS gets healed in the name of Jesus. I cannot remember each and every one that we have prayed for with AIDS, but we have seen the good Lord healing AIDS.

~*~*~

CHILD HEALED OF AIDS

A three year old child, an orphan whose parents had both died of AIDS, was brought to us for prayer. The child was living in agony. We prayed and prayed and prayed.

The child was taken back for tests after one month. The sickness had disappeared. The blood tested negative. The child was completely and totally healed. This child is now over twelve years old. She was healed of AIDS.

~*~*~

"My brother and sister, the power of Jesus Christ to heal sickness is still the same even today. I have seen many healings. In every meeting we conduct, people come with all kinds of diseases. In some places in Uganda you cannot find a clinic. Malaria and many other diseases cannot be treated and the people are left to die.

However, we minister to these people and give them hope. We tell them what Jesus can do in their lives. They open up their hearts and accept the Lord. We have seen Jesus touching them and healing them totally.

We have gone to hospitals and prisons. We have gone to many different places in our country. The good Lord has raised up people who were suffering with all kinds of sicknesses. No matter what kind of sickness, no matter what kind of disease, it gets healed in the name of Jesus Christ.

I have seen tumors disappear. I have seen cancer healed, AIDS healed, and leukemia healed. I have seen all kinds of pain and disease healed in the name of Jesus Christ." - Pastor Kaweesa

ENLARGED STOMACH HEALED

We went to a village to minister in a type of revival meeting. There, I saw something very unusual happen to a young girl. This young girl had a very abnormal tummy. It was so huge! The devil had deformed her.

The father told me that they had tried all kinds of hospitals and had tried many medications on her. But, the tummy was only continuing to expand. I had never seen such a big, enormous tummy on a young girl like that. She was only seven years of age. She was in much agony and pain and was crying and screaming.

I told the father that we believe in the God who does miracles, and that we believe in the God who delivers people. I knew that this kind of situation was a type of demonic influence, that there was some kind of spirit behind it. That is how God revealed it to me.

So, we laid our hands upon this young girl and rebuked the evil spirit in the name of Jesus Christ. We then encouraged the father and mother that this girl was healed in the name of Jesus. I encouraged them to send us a report of what had taken place. They went home.

After some weeks had passed, we received a wonderful report. They told us that certain smelly fluids began coming out of the girl's belly day after day. And, as that happened, the tummy just went down, went down, went down. She is now doing very fine. They are all very thankful to the Almighty God. They are very, very happy.

~*~*~

PREGNANT FOR TWO YEARS

There was a woman who came to me who said she had been pregnant for two years, but failed to deliver. She said that every time she went to the hospital to deliver, the womb disappeared. I saw this lady and she appeared to be pregnant. Her tummy was very big. When she explained how for two years she had been having this pregnancy, I could not understand it. I asked why she was not operated on. She said that every time she went to the hospital, they could not find the child.

I opened my Bible and shared with this lady the miracle working power of God. I shared with her how Jesus came to save and heal no matter what kind of sickness. She accepted Christ. We then prayed together, and in the name of Jesus, I rebuked that evil spirit. I charged that demon to leave her in Jesus' name. Then, I said, "In the name of Jesus, if the child is there, I pray that the child may grow." And, the lady left.

She continued to come to our services. Two months went by and she went to the hospital. The doctors saw a child in her and gave her medication. After another two months time, she felt labor pain, went to the hospital and delivered a child who was a boy.

This boy had hair all over his body. The hair was thick and his skin was very dark. He looked like a monkey. We went and prayed for her and the child. They discharged her from the hospital. After about six months, the thick hair on the child began to disappear and his body was fully restored to that of a child. The child continued to grow. God performs miracles!

~*~*~

WOMAN DELIVERS HEALTHY BABY

A woman came to us crying and in a lot of pain. She said that she had been pregnant for a year and a half. We shared the Word of the Lord with her and she became born-again. We, then, prayed together. She went home and began to get labor pains. She went to the hospital and delivered a baby girl. This baby girl was very fine. We thanked God together.

Remember, that God is able to perform miracles for any person. The devil had taken captive their tummies. He had caused them a lot of pain. That kind of witchcraft is very prevalent here in Uganda and in many parts of Africa. But, the name of Jesus is able to free those people from that kind of demonic influence.

~*~*~

"Many women that have been unable to conceive have come for prayer. If a lady in Africa fails to conceive, it is a very, very big problem. It is taboo. It is believed very strongly that if a woman fails to have children, she is not needed in the home. Why should she go on eating food for nothing? So, these ladies suffer a lot.

In my ministry, I have been on the frontlines to pray for these ladies who have been abused in such a manner. We have prayed for them and believed God together. God is faithful and loving. He is able to open up such wombs and cast away that evil spirit of barrenness. I have seen God perform miracles in their lives." - Pastor Kaweesa

SPIRIT OF BARRENNESS CAST OUT

One time I was invited to minister at a church which had about four hundred people. As I was preaching the Lord guided my eyes to look at a particular lady. God told me to call her forward. I instructed her, "Come with your husband."

As they came forward, the Lord told me that they had been married for seven years, but they had failed to have children. So, I called for other ministers and we prayed for this couple in the name of Jesus Christ. We cast out that evil spirit of barrenness. Within one month, the lady conceived. She was able to deliver a beautiful baby boy!

I thank God for that. Jesus can perform any miracle in any person's life in any place on this planet! The Lord is able to perform miracles!

~*~*~

LIKE SARAH AND HANNAH

There was another lady who had been married for ten years and who was unable to conceive. She was very disturbed. The clan of the husband was unhappy with her. The sister and the brothers of the husband were telling him to chase her away.

This particular woman came weeping and crying. She had spent ten years in that marriage. The husband was always encouraging his wife and telling her, "I love you. I love you, my wife. You are my wife. I know that it is God who gives children." Although the husband was not born-again, he believed that it is God that gives children.

I shared with this lady about Sarah from the Bible, and how she was able to deliver even when she was very, very old. I also shared how Hannah was able to deliver when she cried out to the Lord. Then, I told her, "You have come to the right place. God is able to help you. Our God is able to open up your womb and He is able to enable you to conceive." We prayed with her. She was

203

able to conceive and she delivered a very beautiful baby girl within one year! They brought the baby to me and I was very thankful to the Lord. We glorified the Lord.

~*~*~

"My dear sister, our God is a God of miracles! There is a miracle for you! Maybe as you are reading this, you are barren. The Lord is able to open up your womb and enable you to conceive, in Jesus' name. I encourage you, believe God!" - Pastor Kaweesa

Question & Answer

Q: Pastor Kaweesa, how did come to know that you were used in the healing ministry?

A: When I had just become saved and accepted Jesus Christ as my personal Savior, I was impressed when I saw the sick prayed for in my church, and when I saw devils being cast out. I remember hearing the testimonies of what the Lord had done for them. I had never heard of that before in my life. I took that serious.

My first experience in being used in healing was when I prayed for the young Muslim girl who was in a coma in my parent's village. The Lord raised her up and many came to the Lord. I was very encouraged, and determined to search out the scriptures and to pray for the sick. I started to visit the hospital. This was outside of the church program; I did it on my own spare time.

In the hospital I continued to see miracle healing. I said, "I have to go to those who are very, very sick, to those whom the doctors have given up." I went to the hospital and asked the doctors, "Please, I want to pray for those

who are very, very sick." So, they took me to them and I saw the healing power of Jesus Christ.

I was taken to one lady who was dying of cancer. She could not talk, she couldn't do anything. I prayed a prayer of faith and believed God. The next day when I went back, that lady was normal. She could talk. They told her, "This is the young man who prayed for you." She was very, very thankful. She got born-again. I told her, "Jesus loves you." Within one week, that lady was discharged from the hospital, after having been in the hospital one complete year.

And Jesus went about all their cities and villages,
teaching in their synagogues,
preaching the gospel of the kingdom,
and healing every sickness
and disease among the people.
Matthew 9:35

~*~

Jesus Christ is the same yesterday,
today and forever. Hebrews 13:8

~*~

And the prayer of faith will save the sick,
and the Lord will raise him up.
And if he has committed any sins,
he will be forgiven. James 5:15

Steven Kaweesa

~ Thirteen ~

GIFTS OF THE SPIRIT

*Now we have received not the
spirit of the world,
but the Spirit which is from God,
that we might understand the
gifts bestowed on us by God.
I Corinthians 2:12*

Steven Kaweesa

"God gives different gifts to His ministers. These gifts are much needed in the world today. One of those is prophecy. In my ministry the Lord has given me prophetic messages for places, homes, individuals and villages.

Sometimes, the Lord uses me in this area in church services, as well as when I am counseling. The Lord will give me the right word for the people. I have seen, as the Lord has allowed me to operate in this gift, that it has helped people to come out of their problems and areas where they are deceived." - Pastor Kaweesa

MARRIAGE RESTORED

A lady came to me for counseling in 1976. Her problem was that her marriage was falling apart. Her husband had left her. She came crying and explained how her husband had different women and how he was living with another woman. She talked at length about the evils of the man. She told me that she didn't think she had any wrong in her life, except for when she became angry about some small things.

I shared with her how she may have some things that she needed to make right. I explained how God is loving and kind and how God is able to help her so that her marriage may be restored. She was not born-again. I shared with her and told her we would pray. She closed her eyes and knelt down.

During the counseling session I had asked her, "Now, you don't have any boyfriends?"

She answered me, "No. I don't have any boyfriends. I have been faithful to my husband."

As I was about to pray for her, the Holy Spirit told me, "Don't pray for her. This lady is deceiving you. She has a boyfriend right at her place of work. She has been living in adultery a long time."

So, I said, "Lady, you came here to be helped by God. If you deceive me, try to understand, that God knows you well. Why have you deceived me? You have a boyfriend right at the place of your work."

As I spoke that, this lady went right down on the floor and began shaking. I got her hand and raised her up. I said, "Lady, be at peace. I am not here to threaten you. God is here to help you out of your problems. You need to repent and tell the Lord that you have done evil, and repent for adultery and trying to deceive the Lord, and turn." She did that as we prayed together.

I tell you, God is so miraculous! In three days after our prayer, the husband came back to the home. The husband repented to her and she repented to her husband. Their home was restored.

~*~*~

FOUR YEAR OLD RACHEL PROTECTED FROM A PYTHON

On a Wednesday I was conducting a small service. The Lord spoke to me, "There is a parent whose child is going to face a python, but I will guard that child from the python." I didn't know which parent the Lord was speaking about, but I was encouraged that the Lord was going to guard the child.

Two weeks later, a brother came to service and gave a testimony. He said that one day he had returned home, but his wife was not yet home from her job. They have three children, and one of them is a girl called Rachel, who is four years of age.

Behind their house is a big plantation of banana trees. Here in Uganda, we eat a lot of bananas. It is a very important food for us. This particular plantation was about two acres of bananas. When the father came home, he did not find the children, so he went behind the house because he knew that they sometimes play back there.

In the garden, he found two of his children, and asked them, "Where is your sister?"

The two children said, "She has gone in that direction, and she has gone with a cart."

The father went calling, "Rachel, Rachel, Rachel!" At last he heard a voice say, "Yes, here I am."

When he was about to reach Rachel, he saw her standing, and in front of her was a large python! The python had strangled the cart that Rachel had been pulling, and was attempting to swallow the cart. Rachel was standing there watching and ordering the python, "You leave the cart! You leave the cart!"

The father was so much afraid that he jumped, grabbed Rachel, ran away and made an alarm. They brought spears and killed that big, enormous python.

Rachel was saved. God spared her life. God's hand was right there. God speaks to His people. The Lord did just as He had spoken, "I am going to take care of her; I am going to guard her from the python." Rachel was completely and totally protected. Praise the Lord!

~*~*~

SEED OF OBEDIENCE RELEASES A MIRACLE

While I was ministering on a Wednesday, the Lord showed me a woman and told me to have her stand up. She stood up. The Lord told me that she had bought a dress some days ago. He wanted her to give away that dress, and if she would be obedient to do that, her miracle would be released. So, I told her that and prayed over her.

She went and told her husband. He said, "Yes, give it away. If the Lord has spoken, give it away." So, the Lord showed her which sister to give the dress to, which she did. She later told me how she had struggled to buy that dress.

It so happened that the sister who gave the dress away was a government teacher and the school district officers that she was working for, were embezzling school fees and were not paying the teachers their full salaries. Some teachers never ended up being paid at all. They only survived on the little money they received from the parents. This particular teacher had not been getting paid her salary for one year and two months. She was only living on the little money that the parents were giving. And yet, she didn't want to lose a government job.

The day after she had given her dress away, a paycheck came in the mail for one complete year and two months pay. She had given up on that money. She knew it had been embezzled and that she would never get her money at all. When she received her check, she could not believe her eyes! She was very grateful. She was very thankful!

She came and gave us her testimony and thanked God so much. God is very, very good.

~*~*~

"Whenever God says to do something, please obey the Living God. Be obedient and you will be blessed." - Pastor Kaweesa

DISOBEDIENCE: THE FRUIT OF A REBELLIOUS HEART

As I was counseling one day, a sister came whom I had never seen before. She sat down. The Lord told me that she had come to get prayed for, that she was going to get married.

The Lord told me to tell her that the man she was going to marry was not born-again, and that the marriage would only last five years. The Lord showed me that this man was ungodly, and that they had already fallen into sin and had committed fornication many times. I prayed that God would help to encourage and restore this sister.

I said to her, "So, you have come for the purpose of marriage."

She answered, "Yes,"

I told her, "You know that the man you are going to get married to is not born-again."

She again answered, "Yes."

I inquired of her, "Yet, you are born-again?"

Again, she said, "Yes."

I told her, "You, as a born-again, have not only decided to marry this man, but you have fallen into fornication a number of times. Do you know that you are living in sin right now?"

She answered, "Yes."

I asked her, "What can you do about that?"

She replied, "I am very sorry. I am repenting."

I advised her, "Let me tell you what. You may get married, but your marriage will only last five years. What do you say about that?"

She said, "I am repenting, may God forgive me."

She knelt down and we prayed. As we were praying, the Lord told me that she was going to go ahead and get married to that man. I kept that to myself. I prayed and begged God that this sister would change her heart and turn to God completely.

Such people do come. Some come when they are ready to change and do the right thing. They hear God's

Word and they are ready to change. However, there are also those who are not ready to change. Even when they hear God's Word, they are not ready to change at all. And, such was this sister, who was not ready to change at all. She left and I have never seen her again.

...Believe in the Lord your God,
and you shall be established;
Believe His prophets,
and you shall prosper
2 Chronicles 20:20

~*~*~

OBEDIENCE BRINGS BLESSING

A very helpless lady came to us. She had a lot of debts and no job at that time. We get many people of this nature, who do not have a job. They are helpless. Sometimes, if you have a little money in your pocket, you have to give it to help this kind of person.

"In Uganda, here where I am serving, we as ministers find that the little bit of salary that we get, we oftentimes have to spend and give it back. Time and again, needy people come to us, and the church doesn't have that kind of money to give out. So, we hear the Lord tell us to give and we do that faithfully as the Lord provides." - Pastor Kaweesa

This lady explained all her problems. I didn't have any money, but we serve a wonderful Lord. As I prayed with this lady, the Lord spoke to me and said, "Tell this lady to go to the city tomorrow morning and I will give her a job right there."

She had been looking for a job for about two years. She had looked everywhere. She was not an invalid. So, I told her, as the Lord had instructed, "Lady, tomorrow morning, get a taxi and go to the city and the Lord is going to give you a job."

She asked me, "When I reach the city, what am I to do? Which side should I go to?"

I didn't have the answer, but as she was speaking, the voice of the Lord spoke to me and said, "Tell her to get in the taxi and go to the taxi park. And in the taxi park, there are ladders. Tell her to go to the ladders, and I will show her what I am going to do." So, I told her that.

In the morning, she got a taxi, went to the taxi park, and then went to the ladders. As she was finishing climbing the ladders, a woman met her whom she had not seen in a long time. They greeted each other. The woman then said, "I have been looking for you! I have a job for you. It is a place of serving drinks and food. You can run the place."

Our sister was very thankful! She then ran into another lady who wanted her to come to work, also. But, she remembered that the Lord had told her that He would show her a job on the ladders, so, she stayed with that job. She has now been on that job for the last twenty years. God is very faithful!

~*~*~

GOD PROTECTS WOMAN'S SCHOOL

A lady came very early to my house at about six o'clock in the morning. The children, who were getting ready for school, opened for her and called me. I had never seen this lady before. I didn't know how she came to know my house. She began crying and crying. I didn't say anything at that time, but walked back to my bedroom and sat on my bed.

I asked the Lord, "Why is that lady crying like that? I understand she has a big problem, but what kind of problem is it? Lord, can you help me? Tell me the problem, and give me the solution for this lady."

Instantly, the Lord spoke to me, and said, "This lady has a school which is having a big problem right now. Certain men have tried to forge documents to steal away her school. Go and tell her that I have taken all those problems and that no one is going to take her school. Let her be at peace."

So, I went to her. She was still sobbing and crying. I said, "Lady, you have a school and your school is in a big problem right now. There are certain men who are trying to steal away your school. They have forged papers, is that right?"

Her eyes were wide open. She looked at me. The tears dried up, and she said, "Yes. Yes, Pastor."

I went on and said, "Lady, the Lord is saying to you that no one is going to take your school. The school is yours and no one is going to take it. Be at peace, okay?" She was very, very thankful. I told her to kneel down, raise her hands and give thanks to God. We gave thanks together and she left.

After seven days, she came back and gave me a testimony of how the Lord had fought her battle. Her enemies turned and repented to her. The school was restored to her. She went on with her job.

~*~*~

"God is so good. He can fight for you. He knows how to fight and win. He will never lose any battle. He is there to help you out at any time." - Pastor Kaweesa

GOD WARNS OF DANGER IN SOFA

It is my practice to go and visit the people's homes. One particular time, I had gone to visit an elderly woman's home. She was there and gave me a seat. It was a type of old sofa.

I sat down and as she finished greeting me, I heard the Lord tell me, "Steve, get out of that seat!"

I asked, "Lord, why? She has given me this seat."

The Lord commanded again, "Get out of that seat!"

I decided to stay, and the Lord spoke to me a third time, "Get out of that seat!"

I finally said, "Yes, Lord, okay."

I told the lady, "Lady, the Lord has told me to get out of this seat and I don't think that I'm going to sit anywhere. It seems that your house has a problem. I feel that I have to go."

As I was leaving, she said, "Don't go, don't go." But, I continued going. When I reached outside, I heard her shout at the top of her voice, "Pastor, it's a snake! It's a snake!" She shouted so loud that it even alarmed the neighbors to come and see what was taking place. She had looked in that old sofa, and do you know what was in there? A big snake came out of that ugly old sofa seat!

We got a stick and killed that snake. It was a deadly snake, very poisonous. People ran to see. After we had killed the snake, I preached about salvation and people got born-again. God is so good. It was because of His voice, my life was spared. If He had not spoken, then maybe that snake would have bitten me on my back. Our God is very, very good!

~*~*~

WOMAN REPENTS FOR SPEAKING AGAINST THE MEN OF GOD

I went down to minister at the Redeemed Church at a revival meeting that was to run for three days. I was to preach every day.

As I stood to minister, the Lord told me, "See that lady? Tell her to stand up." I told her, and she stood up. The Lord then told me, "That lady has three schools, but one school has given her a lot of trouble and she is considering closing it. Tell her that she should not close that school; I have restored it and have taken away all

219

the problems in that school." So, that is what I told her. Then, I instructed her to raise her hands, and I prayed for her concerning the schools. I then went ahead with the Word of the Lord, after which I prayed for a number of people, including those needing deliverance.

After about two weeks, this lady came to me and said, "Pastor Steve, you helped me. God can speak. That problem at my school had been there for a long time. I was very discouraged. I had prayed and prayed and didn't seem to get an answer. So, what I did was I moved from church to church, especially in those churches where I knew that the men of God get revelation from God. I sat in their congregations waiting for the Lord to speak something to me. I wanted it directly from the pastor, for him to stand up and say to me, 'Lady, you have such and such a problem.'

I went to four churches and they called different people, but they never called me. I came to the conclusion that these pastors are liars, that God never speaks like that. I believed that these men just line up people whom they know very well and then they speak words to deceive people into thinking that it is God who is speaking, and it's not God, it's just men trying to manufacture those words.

But, then you spoke those words to me. We had a night prayer for our ladies, but I spent the whole night crying and repenting of the evil thoughts and words I had spoken against the men of God, and against God. I asked God to forgive me, and now, Pastor, I have come here. I know that God can speak. I know that God knows me very well."

That was a turning point in that lady's life. All the problems in her school disappeared and went away completely.

God can speak.

~*~*~

"The Lord gives the prophetic ministry to the church to edify and encourage, to uplift and build up. Even personally, this gift is very helpful. Many times the Lord has given a word for my children. Many of these words have come to pass and some prophecies are still in the near future to come. God is very good." - Pastor Kaweesa

GOD KNOWS ALL THE DETAILS

I had gone to minister in a church that was north of the city. This was during Idi Amin's rule. It was an "overnight" meeting where about twenty-five people were gathered. As the meeting started, I sensed a spirit of fear that was covering everyone there. It was holding the whole congregation captive. The Spirit of the Lord told me to listen, and He began to reveal to me things about every person in that room. Some of it was about needs they had in their lives, some of it dealt with fear they were experiencing. There was one very notable miracle that happened that night.

A gentleman had a wife that had been gone for six months. When she left, she was only going to be gone for two weeks to see her parents in a village 160 miles away. He was very worried. He was a poor man; he didn't have the means to go anywhere, and no telephone. He didn't know what to do. His wife was gone and he loved her so much. She had taken the two children.

The Lord showed me his situation, which I told him about, and he said, "Yes." I told him to kneel down and we would pray. I encouraged him to believe God. He knelt down. As we were just going to pray, the Lord told me, "Don't pray. His wife has come back."

I told the man, "We don't need to pray. Your wife has come back. You just go ahead and thank God." But, in my spirit, I was wondering, "Lord, the wife is back? How could she come back from 160 miles away?"

That morning as the man went back to his house, the wife was right at the door waiting. As he looked at his wife, he could not believe his eyes. He was so happy! He ran back to the church shouting, "The wife is back! God is good!" We all thanked God for that wonderful, great miracle.

~*~*~

BUSINESSMAN BELIEVES GOD

One day the Lord told me to go to town and meet a man called Emanuel, a born-again businessman. He had been praying, but I didn't know what he had been praying for as he was in a different church, not ours.

As I went to him, the Lord showed me that He had given this man land in the city of Kampala. The Lord told me that Emanuel was going to be able to build a very large complex of buildings, and that these buildings would house business places, a school, and offices. The Lord gave me a vision of those buildings. It was huge.

I went to town and shared this with Emanuel. He said, "You are a true pastor. I have been praying and asking God to give me a place in this town. I have been asking God to give me a building. I don't have money other than a little money to run my business. Land is very expensive. I would have to spend three or four hundred million shillings, maybe even five hundred or more. Whenever I think about that, it's very difficult for me. But, yet, I believe and pray."

I told him to just begin to give thanks to God. "The Lord has given you that land," I assured him.

Do you know what happened? Within three weeks time, when Emanuel was at his business, a lady came to purchase cement. Emanuel was with another brother loudly sharing the Word of God. This lady was with the cashier and heard the words which he was sharing. She turned, came to him, and asked, "Are you born-again?"

He answered her, "Yes, I am born-again."

She was very excited and said, "I am just visiting. I live in Nigeria. I have been in Nigeria for twenty years. I came to see my people, but also, I have come to sell my land which I have in this city of Kampala. I am also born-again and since you are born-again, I want to sell this land to you. Will you buy it?"

Emanuel just said, "Yes, yes, yes!"

They made an arrangement and they went to the land. My, the land was big. It was two acres of land in the city of Kampala, the biggest city in our country of Uganda. Understand this, for just one acre in the city of Kampala, you can spend even more than five hundred million.

While Emanuel waited to hear how much he would have to give, instead of a hundred million, two or three hundred million, four or five hundred million, or a billion, this lady said, "I want forty million."

Emanuel could not believe it! The lady said, "You're free to take your time. I'm here for two months. You go and find the money. I'm not going to sell it to another person. I'm born-again. I just want to bless you as a child of God."

My, Emanuel was so excited! He ran and looked for that forty million Uganda shilling. Not dollars, it's Uganda shilling.

Emanuel came to me and told me about his wonderful miracle. He asked me, "Do you know what I am going to do now?"

I answered, "No, what are you going to do?"

He said, "Well, I have my car, and I am going to try to sell it to start putting something up."

I advised him, "My brother, selling your car is not what the Lord showed me. It is like you are pouring a bucket of water into the ocean. It doesn't make any difference. So, just keep your car and the good Lord who has given you this land, is going to bless you. He is going to bless your work in a way you have never even imagined."

He listened and took my word. And, do you know what? The Lord blessed his business. A big construction company came to him and they made a deal with him to supply them with tons and tons of cement. He went to the bank to borrow the money and he started supplying those tons and tons of cement. He made huge profits. He got the money and paid for the land. He then came to take me to see the land. When I reached there, I saw it and prayed.

Today, there is a building on the land, and he is even expanding that complex. There is a secondary school, which is called a Najja High School, and there are also other businesses.

The Lord is so good. The Lord can speak, and whatever the Lord speaks is right. The Lord is always right.

~*~*~

GOD RESURRECTS WOMAN'S BUSINESS

Another time when I was in my office doing counseling, a lady came to me whom I had never seen before. The Lord spoke to me, "This lady has come from Entebbe." Entebbe is twenty miles from where I live.

The Lord went on to tell me, "This lady has a business that has run bankrupt, but tell her that I am resurrecting her business today."

I told her what the Lord had told me and she was very, very excited and thankful to God. The Lord did indeed resurrect her business, and even today, as far as I know, her business is going on well.

~*~*~

"The Lord is able to resurrect even those things which you think are dead in your life. God can bring them

225

back. He is able. Whatever God says is always true." - Pastor Kaweesa

WILL YOU LIE TO THE ONE WHO FORMED THE EYES AND EARS?

There was a lady who had become born-again back in the seventies and it had been about twelve or thirteen years since I had seen her. She came, looking wonderful.

She said, "Pastor Steve, praise the Lord!" I was very happy to see her and she was very happy to see me. She had come with a young man. When we sat down, she started explaining the business she had been dealing in. She told me that her business was very large, but that she had run into a little trouble and she needed some money. She wanted me to loan her money. I didn't have any money to loan her.

In my spirit, as she was speaking, I was praying, "Lord, it has been thirteen years since I have seen this sister and now she comes wanting money. God, I don't have any money. Can you give me the right answer for this lady?"

As I was praying, the Lord spoke right away to me. Do you know what He revealed to me? I'm going to tell you. The Lord told me that this lady had a lot of debts and that one of the largest debts she owed was over a million shilling. She had wanted me to loan her 100,000 Uganda shilling. (Our money is big in volume, but it is not big in purchase power.) As the Lord showed me about all her debts, I thanked Him for showing me the situation.

I asked this sister, "If I give you 100,000 is that enough to solve all your problems, to pay all your debts?"

"Yes," she replied.

"Okay." I continued, "Now, do you know that you have a lot of debts and that one of the biggest debts you have is one million shilling? Do you know that?"

She was very quiet. And, in a low voice, she replied, "Yes."

I went on to say, "Now, do you think that 100,000 shilling is going to solve all your problems? What I want to do is give you information that will help you to not only get the 100,000, but to get the whole amount you need to pay all your debts. You have even dodged the people you owe money. You don't want to see them. They have come to you time and time again and you have run away from them."

She said, "Yes, Pastor."

I opened the Bible and shared with her how the Lord could enable her to pay her debts. I advised her how to do business right, and how to make friends, not enemies. I shared with her for quite a long time.

At last, I said, "Okay, sister, we are going to pray and believe God for you that He may enable you to come out of all those debts."

As I was about to lay hands on her to pray, the Lord commanded me, "Don't lay hands on her! This lady is no longer seeking blessings from Me, she is going to witchdoctors." She had backslid. I prayed within my heart, "Lord, help me to bring back this lost sheep."

So, I said, "Lady, you have already backslid and you go to the witchdoctors. Tell me every witchdoctor you have visited." She began mentioning one after another, over five in all. She was going to them seeking blessings.

I said, "Oh, sister, you have backslid."

She was crying and shaking. I opened the Bible and shared with her a long time, then told her to repent. She confessed, repented and came back to the Lord. I prayed for her and even the young man who came with her got born-again.

I knew that the Lord led her to me to help her. She came back to the Lord, Jesus Christ. Praise the Lord. God speaks to His people.

To one is given in and through the Holy Spirit
the power to speak a message of wisdom,
To another the power to express a word of
knowledge and understanding
according to the same Holy Spirit;
To another wonder-working faith
by the same Holy Spirit,
To another the extraordinary powers
of healing by the one Spirit;
To another the working of miracles,
To another prophetic insight
(the gift of interpreting the
divine will and purpose);

To another, the ability to discern
and distinguish between the utterances
of true spirits and the false ones,
To another various kinds of unknown tongues,
To another the ability to interpret such tongues.
All these gifts, achievements, and abilities
are inspired and brought to pass by
one and the same Holy Spirit, Who apportions to
each person individually as He chooses
1 Corinthians 12: 8 - 11 AMP

~ *Fourteen* ~

OBSTACLES TO THE FAITH

Watch,
stand fast in the faith,
be brave, be strong.
1 Corinthians 16:13

Steven Kaweesa

"While there are some who encourage us, at the same time, there are those who discourage us. People have discouraged me over the years. If it had not been for the hand of God, I would not have stood. Because of Him, I am still standing." - Pastor Kaweesa

BUT, WE ARE STARVING . . .

We had just come out from the underground, and were preaching the gospel. I was pastoring full-time and relying only on the little money that came into the church. I had married in 1978 and started a family. This money was not enough for my family to survive on. My wife needed extra support and attention while she was pregnant.

My father, who was a businessman, called and asked me to help him. He told me that he understood I was a preacher full-time and not working another job, but he asked me to help him once a week by buying things that he needed for his business. That kind of job would only take about four hours. Go get the money, go buy the stuff, then take back the stuff. Also, by helping my father in that way, I hoped that maybe he would be won to Jesus Christ.

However, men from the church told me that a minister of the Gospel could only be at the church praying and reading his Bible. I explained to them that I was faithful to do that, and that in this situation I would only be gone one day a week helping my father. In fact, I would be finished by noon or at the latest two o'clock, then, I would be right back at the church. In addition, my father would be giving me some money, which I needed for my family. It would be a great help for us to survive on.

But, these brothers said, "No, no, no." The elders were called and the counsel of the elders voted a "no confidence" in me.

They said, "Steve, we love you so much, but we cannot stand that you go to help your father once a week. A man of God must be here always, always."

I explained how I had always served faithfully, and was committed to go ahead serving God faithfully. Nevertheless, they stood their ground and said, "No. We cannot continue with you unless you leave helping your father."

I made it very clear to them, "I am here all the time. I understand what you are saying, but for these few hours, I must use them for the betterment of my wife and the child she is carrying. I cannot just stand around and watch my wife dying from hunger. Perhaps she will not even be able to deliver the child."

However, they persisted, and ordered me, "No, you will have to find another way."

I agreed, and said farewell to the church. By the grace of God, I moved from there. Many cried and begged me not to leave, asking me to just plant another church next to this one. I informed them that I could not do that, that this church is God's work and would continue to grow whether I was there or not.

So, we moved from there to another one of the churches we had planted, by then called the Kibuye

Redeemed Church. I went and pastored there. They loved me and allowed me to help my father.

~*~*~

"There are people who will try to discourage you. They will try to confuse you. They will try to make a very small thing into a very big something. You may find yourself wanting to give up and forsake the work of God.

Please, do not forsake God's work! God has called you! God is with you. God is going to uplift you. God will do whatever it takes to see that what He called you to do comes to pass. That is what God has done in my life.

When I am in the mountains climbing, He is on my side. In the valleys, He is on my side. He is always on my side. He is on our side all the time."
- Pastor Kaweesa

WHEN THOSE YOU HELP TURN AGAINST YOU

There was one guy who had no where to live. I invited him to live in a small room behind my house. He came with his family. At that time, we had a little garden of yams. My wife saw how desperate these people were and offered them a small garden space, although she was still using part of it.

One day as my wife was going to the garden, that man jumped and yelled at her, "What are you doing? This is my garden! Who gave it to you?"

That man began talking and spreading rumors to the whole village about how bad we were, and how badly we were treating them. Yet, we had not done any bad things to them, only good. We gave them a place to stay when they had nowhere to go, and offered them some food. He turned against us.

So, this man and his wife were really a big thorn for us all the time we spent with them. We continued to pray and believe God. We were able to move to a different house, and we left them there. We were so happy!

~*~*~

"People we help may turn against us. However, as a man or woman of God, please always remember, that what they have done to you, they have already done it to Jesus Christ, your Master, my Master, our Master.

So, do not be discouraged. Please, get up, in the name of Jesus! If you have given up or left the ministry, go back in the name of Jesus! Go back to doing what you were called to do." - Pastor Kaweesa

DID YOU SAY "FREE HOUSE"?

There was a lady who visited us and saw how we were struggling. We did not even have enough money to pay for our rent. Hardship was great. This lady asked us to come to a home she was caring for that her son had left. I explained to her that we did not have money. She said that she had seen how we were struggling, and she assured us that she wanted us to come and move into this free house.

I agreed by saying, "Okay. Thank you very much." I talked to my wife and she was very excited. We moved into the house.

After we had been in the house one month, this lady who was born-again and loved the Lord came and told us, "Okay, I gave you an allowance of one month, but these following months, you are going to pay."

I asked, "What, Mama?"

She said, "You are going to pay."

I asked her, "Pay what?"

She answered, "You are going to pay rent. Don't you know that you have to pay? I told you that you can live one month and then you shall pay for the rest of the months."

I said, "Mama, I am very sorry, I am so sorry. I didn't hear well. I didn't know what you meant. I didn't know that you wanted money. I told you very clearly that we were struggling to pay for the rent where we were. We felt that you understood that when you offered to us a free house, and you invited us to move into the house. Now, where are we going to get the money? We don't have that kind of money."

She replied, "If you don't have that kind of money, I am very sorry. Move out of this house!" She was very mad at us.

I said, "Lord, forgive us. Lord, forgive us." During that time, my wife had just given birth. We had no money. I had no money to move our things or to start to pay rent somewhere else. Here in our country when you are getting a house for the first time, you have to pay a down payment of three to six months in advance. I didn't have that kind of money anywhere.

I prayed. One dear sister who understood our situation, invited us into her home until the Lord would bless us with our own house. I was so much discouraged. I could not believe that a born-again whom I had ministered to could come and confuse me to that extent. And then, confront me and make me look like a very bad man, a very bad family. It hurt us very much, especially my wife.

However, the Lord taught us to forgive and reconcile. We moved on. We got a house of our own and we went ahead with our ministry.

~*~*~

"Please do not be discouraged by people. Forgive them. Be encouraged by God. Get God's word and rise up in the name of Jesus!" - Pastor Kaweesa

FELLOW MINISTER BACKSLIDES

There was a minister whom I met during my first year of salvation who encouraged me greatly. After four years, I began to wonder about him, as I had not seen him for quite some time. He was no longer coming to visit us. So, I went to see the man who this minister stayed with whenever he came this way, and inquired of his whereabouts.

That man gave me a very shocking answer. He asked me, "Don't you know? Have they not told you what he did?"

I answered, "No. No one has ever told me and I want to know. What's wrong? What happened?"

This man explained to me how that minister had forsaken the gospel. Not only that, he brought in nine women. Nine women! He was now living with nine women. My, that shook my heart!

The man went on to say, "He has even acquired demonic spirits."

I said, "Oh, my God. He is now a witchdoctor?"

This man answered, "Yes."

The minister whom I had looked up to and greatly admired was now a witchdoctor with nine women. I cried tears. I shed tears. I was very much confused. I was very much troubled. I opened my Bible, but I could not see any scripture that was giving me an answer. My heart was having many questions. I put my Bible aside.

That night as I went home to my bedroom, I was very much depressed. I felt that God could not do that. At that moment, I did not understand who had done wrong to that minister. I thought with my simple knowledge, that it was God who had brought this entire calamity upon him.

I said, "God, You cannot do this to such a man! If You have done this to someone who has been serving You with such a powerful anointing, then as for me, I do not want to be ashamed like that. I have just started serving You, it has just been four years. I do not want the time to come after I have served you that I get those evil spirits and nine women. Lord, just let me stop here!"

I put my Bible aside, saying, "I will never preach the gospel again. And, I will never go back to the church again. From now on, I have decided to go my way. God, leave me alone!" And, I slept.

But, God is so wonderful. Deep in my sleep, the Lord gave me a night vision. In this vision, I heard a voice calling me. It called me by my African name, *Kaweesa*, three times.

"Kaweesa ... Kaweesa ... Kaweesa!"

I answered, "Yes, my Lord, Jesus."

Then, He asked me, "Who called you in salvation?"

I answered, "It's You, my Lord, Jesus."

Then the voice told me, "Look to Me. Do not look to people." When I heard that, I jumped up and ran out of the bedroom. I was so much afraid. I thought that the Lord was going to kill me because I had forsaken Him. I knelt right down on the floor and cried and cried.

I prayed, "Oh, God, forgive me! I am a sinner. I did foolish. Lord, I didn't know what I was doing." I repented before the Almighty God, and as I did, peace came back to me. I was completely restored.

From that time, that voice comes back to me. Who called me? It is my Lord Jesus. If people discourage me, that voice comes back to me saying, "Look to Me; I am your Savior. Look to Me; I am your Redeemer."

~*~*~

WHEN SHEPHERDS BECOME WOLVES

As I was preaching in a different church, the Lord directed me to a certain young girl in her twenties. As I looked at her, the Lord spoke to me, "That girl has a problem. Unless you sit down with her and counsel her, that problem cannot go away."

I went on and preached, but in my heart, I was thinking, "Lord, I came here to visit, I did not come to counsel people. This is not my church." The Lord did not ask me again. So, after I finished preaching I told the pastor that I needed that girl to come to the office so that I could share with her what the Lord had told me.

We made an appointment and she came to the church. As she sat in the office, the Lord gave me this word to tell her, "There is no problem or situation which the Lord cannot solve. God is able to solve every problem and situation for those who come to Him with an open heart."

I asked this girl, "Please, tell me your problem. And, please don't hide anything. The Lord is here to help you."

She told me her story. She said, "Pastor, I had just finished my schooling and I was serving my church faithfully. I was in the choir. But, one day the pastor told me to go to his office and meet with him. He told me that he had seen something in the spirit and that there was a certain problem that was going to come upon me. So, we made an appointment and I went to his office.

When I reached his office, instead of the pastor telling me the problem, he got the anointing oil and anointed me. He then told me to take off all my clothes. I took them off, all of them. He then came out of his seat and raped me right there in his office. I was so afraid. I could not make an alarm, because I feared this pastor so much. After he had finished raping me, he sent me away.

I was staying with my brother. After one month, I discovered that I was pregnant. I came back and told the pastor that I was now pregnant. He told me in a very angry voice with a very ugly face, "Get out from here! I don't want to see you in my office again! And, I don't even want to see you again in our church!"

I was so much embarrassed and confused. I didn't want to tell my brother, because he was the one helping me. I ran away from my brother's home and went to the village of my grandma. I knew that my grandma loved me. When I reached her I explained everything to her and she said to me, 'Okay, my daughter, stay here.' So, I stayed with my grandma."

There are a lot of young girls here in our country that are abused by men. They are abused time and time again. Such was the case with this young girl.

Nine months went by and she was able to deliver a baby boy. After delivering, she brought the baby boy to her pastor to get a name, but the pastor chased her away. So, she went back crying to her grandma. She then named this young boy the name of the pastor.

After that, this girl completely fell away from the Lord. She found another man and conceived. When she found that she was pregnant, she thought, "My first pregnancy was for the pastor and he couldn't help me. Now, what about this guy?"

So, she decided to make an abortion. As she was trying to make an abortion, she got into terrible trouble, and she was dying. The grandma found her and sent a message to the brother, who came and took her to get medical help. They operated on her and saved her life and she recovered.

After all that, the brother encouraged this young girl to come back to the Lord. So, the service she came to was that first service where she had just come back to the Lord, and I called her to come to my office.

She asked me a question, "Can God really forgive me? A pastor slept with me right in his office. I made an abortion. Can God really forgive me?"

Within my heart, I was crying as I prayed, "Oh, God! How can a pastor do such evil things to the people that he is leading?" It was very hard for me; I could not stomach it. Yet, I was in a place where I must help this young girl and to encourage her. I had to guard my emotions. I had to guard my tears. I had to be firm. I had to speak the word of God to help this young girl. I knew she was in this kind of big trouble. She was traumatized, but I knew that the word of the Lord could restore her. There are no psychiatrists in this country that I know of. We pastors do this kind of work.

I opened the word of the Lord and shared with her how Jesus can forgive sins and how He is so caring and loving. The Lord restored the mind of this sister. She was crying and crying, but at last, she regained her strength. We prayed with her. She was very happy and thankful to God as she left.

God is so good. If God had not given me that word, how would I have discovered the trouble in this young girl's life? It was because of God's voice. God speaks to people. Even today, He can speak to you.

~*~*~

MORE WOLVES . . .

As I was visiting and ministering in a church, the Lord showed me a lady that I must speak to. Her name was Janet. We made an appointment.

Before Janet could share anything, I spoke to her, "The Lord is so good. The Lord is so loving. The Lord is very caring. The Lord is forgiving." He had already showed me that this lady was in a very big problem.

I invited her, "Please sister, go ahead and share with me. What is your problem?"

Janet shared how she had a good job. She had been saved for the last eight years. Before she had been saved she ran with different men. Since the time of her salvation, she had guarded herself from all kinds of evil. She got away from all those men, and during those eight years, she had never slept with any men. Janet was waiting on the Lord.

A minister of the Lord began coming to her office. It was a kind of friendship, but it wasn't a kind of serious friendship where someone is trying to engage you. No, it was just like someone who is coming to visit the flock and encourage his sheep. That's how it was.

One day when the pastor went to this sister's job, there was no other person there. Janet was in the office by herself. They talked and talked. What she didn't know was that this minister, a man of God, a man who is called to preach the gospel, a man who fears God, is having a very different intention. His intention was to harm this sister.

As Janet was getting up from her chair to use the restroom, this man followed her, got a hold of her and raped her. After he did that, she was very bitter. He threatened her, "Now you have to marry me. If you don't marry me, you are going to die! And, if you speak of this to any person, know that at that time, you are going to die."

Can you imagine? A man who is regarded as a man of God, one who is respected and is thought to give God's Word in difficult situations, is going on planting corruption. He goes on planting poison. That was poison!

Janet was very much confused. She was very disturbed. She couldn't confess this to anyone, not even to her pastor. She kept quiet. The man continued to come and threaten her, "You have to marry me! You have to marry me!"

Janet backslid and accepted what this man was telling her. She ended up in the house of this man. They had the first child, then the second child. Then, on the third child, it was discovered that this man had AIDS. Janet was very, very frustrated. She became very confused.

She said, "God, how come? I had waited for eight years and this man came and raped me. And this man forced me to marry him. Now he has AIDS. I am going to die. Why, Lord?" Everyday she was crying.

The time came when the man became very sick and he lay dying. He called his pastor, the man he was serving with, and repented and tried to make things right. He called Janet and repented. But, she said, "No. I will never forgive you. You knew what you were doing. You came and raped me knowing that you were sick with AIDS. I will never forgive you. You killed me! I will never forgive you!"

The time came when this man died. And when he died, Janet began hearing within her, "You refused to forgive. Do you think you will ever be forgiven? You are also going to die and you are going to hell. You are going to be in torment for ever and ever." She began suffering psychologically with that kind of questioning going on over and over. So, she repented to her pastors, but she did not tell them what she was suffering from.

Janet had come back to the church, and that's when I met her. As I sat with her, she asked me, "Pastor, is the Lord really able to forgive me? What should I do? Do I have to go to the grave of this man and ask for his forgiveness even though he is dead?"

I answered her, "No, no, you can't do that. But, I tell you this one thing, God can forgive you. God is able to forgive you today. You just need to put your life right. Just say, 'Lord, I am sorry. I did wrong. I didn't forgive.' That man repented before God, and he was forgiven. That man is now in heaven. So, remember, if you don't repent before God, it is your problem. Just repent, and everything will be fine."

Janet repented. I prayed with her that God would lift her spirit up and restore her understanding of the Word of the Lord so that she could do all that she was supposed to do before she got all those problems. And, to love the Lord with all her energy.

Janet was very, very happy. She went away thanking God and praising and glorifying the name of the Lord.

God can speak to His people.

~*~*~

"So, my dear brethren, people may discourage us. But, when you are discouraged, there is hope for you. There is hope for you. Don't give up. Look to Jesus. He is the founder of your faith. He is the finisher of your faith." - Pastor Kaweesa

Therefore we also, since we are surrounded
by so great a cloud of witnesses,
let us lay aside every weight,
and the sin which so easily ensnares us,
and let us run with endurance the race
that is set before us, looking unto Jesus,
the author and finisher of our faith,
who for the joy that was set before Him
endured the cross, despising the shame,
and has sat down at the right
hand of the throne of God."
Hebrews 12: 1-2

~ Fifteen ~

A GOOD REWARD

Two are better than one,
Because they have a good
reward for their labor.
Ecclesiastes 4:9

Steven Kaweesa

LABORERS IN THE HARVEST

After coming to Seguku, I met with Steven Mayanja. He, along with George and his wife, were the only Born-agains in Seguku. They had started a fellowship and were meeting at seven o' clock every evening at George's house to pray for their village and country. My wife and I joined them and we had a wonderful time every evening in prayer.

Also, Steven had started a Children's Church. Every Sunday when he came back from church, he gathered a number of village children together to come and get God's Word. He would buy them candy, and that was a very big thing for the children. Every Sunday the number of children grew!

Then in August of 1984, Steven left for the U.S.A. to attend Bible College, leaving me in his house. My wife, Sarah, took over the Children's Church, and then after a few months, two other young girls joined Sarah to help her. The Children's Church grew.

I started a Friday night service and invited people to attend. They did, and got born-again. Before Steven left for the U.S.A., we had agreed that there was a need to start a church in the village. On my side, I was willing to help Steven start this church, but I didn't have a thought that I would join him to pastor it. I was already doing a good work at the church where I pastored.

In early 1986, Steven wrote and asked me if I would join him in starting a ministry in Uganda. As I prayed about it, the Lord told me, "That is why I brought you to this village." I wrote back with a big "Yes!"

251

So, Steven sent the money and I opened up Uganda Christian Outreach Ministry. Then, in June of that year, Steven came with three others from the U.S. for a short visit. They were Pastor Ron DeVore and his wife, Shirley, and Tom Bales. They stayed for three months, inviting people to come for meetings every day. Many were born-again and Seguku Worship Center was born.

Steven went back to the U.S.A. to finish his degree, and then came back in 1989. I have worked with this man of God all these years.

~*~*~

I first met Ron and Shirley DeVore in 1987 when they came over with Steven Mayanja. They had come with the blessing of their pastor, John Holliday, not knowing what to expect. At that time, Uganda was in a very sorry state. We had just come out of war. The AIDS disease was spreading like wildfire. It was a land of tragedy. Everywhere one looked, there was the pain of war, poverty and the AIDS disease. Many buildings were destroyed by war; a number of industries were not working. Everything was completely in ruins.

When Ron and Shirley arrived, the airport was in a very sorry state. There was no electricity at the airport, so the arrival desk was using candles for light. Also, the car we used to pick them up from the airport broke down a number of times. Ron could not believe what he was seeing. However, instead of getting back on the airplane and going to his country, this man of God really emulated the example of our Lord Jesus Christ. God had already begun to work on their hearts. Ron and Shirley saw a country that needed God. And, Uganda's only hope was to be found in God.

Ron said that as he observed all the ruins of war and disease, he became mad at the devil, and from there, a vision began to grow within him for Uganda. Ron said "yes" to God, but at the same time wondered how he would ever help a country that needed so much. However, Ron is a man whom the Lord called, and Ron took that call.

I have seen some people come to a country such as ours, ruined by war, deep in poverty and disease. And after observing such, they have gotten back on the plane and left for home. They may have intended to stay for a certain time, but within three or four days they left, saying that they could not stomach what they had seen.

I believe that the Lord has called us to face challenges and to go to God's people everywhere He sends us to go.

After a few weeks into Ron's stay, I asked Steven to ask Ron and Shirley if they would be willing to visit Luwero Triangle. This is the area that was so severely damaged by war. It was hell on earth. Kampala was terrible, but one could not believe what had happened to the villages in that particular area. Ron and Shirley accepted, and so we packed thirteen people into our seven-passenger van. That's how it was in those days. Ron must have wondered, "What kind of people are these people?" But, he never said a word.

We traveled into the war triangle and came to the first heap of human bones which were at a level so that one could see the human skulls, thousands of human skulls. The village in this area was known as Matuga. It is about fifteen miles from Kampala on Bombo road. But, that was not all, we continued with our journey. On this road, we came to another village called Kigogwa. There we saw a very large mango tree that had thousands of bones lying around it, and it even had skulls hanging up in the tree. There were also skulls hanging up in the electrical wires, which meant that those people were killed by using electrical wires, and had died in terrible pain.

Anyone who is a visitor to a country at such a time as this would find it difficult to trust the people around you, thinking anyone may be a killer, a murderer. However, no matter how bad this place looked, Ron knew that there were some good people.

We continued on and as we passed by the villages we saw thousands of bones and skulls all over. We drove forty miles and passed by the town of Luwero. It was a ghost town in ruins. Five miles further down Ngoma road we came to a valley of death. There were thousands and thousands of bones and skulls everywhere we looked.

People, who had survived the war, were just coming out of the bush where they had been hiding for five years. Many were almost naked. It was a very, very hard situation. We didn't have any extra clothes to give to these people, except, I remember that Steven had two t-shirts and he gave one to a young thirteen year old boy. The boy was so happy. We thought that he would throw away his rags, but no, he took his rags back.

This was the area where I was born, and my mother and father lived in this area. They had also lived during those years of war in the bush. We went to my parent's home. Everything was ugly. After a long day of seeing nothing but skulls and bones, my heart was heavy. I was wondering how people could do those things to their fellow people.

It was difficult to think about eating, but food had been prepared for us Ugandans and also for the people all the way from the U.S. Traveling through the jungles and looking at the remains of war must have been difficult for Ron and Shirley, seeing all the human bones was not easy, but they just took the food and ate.

After we left there, we came to a small church which a friend of mine had just started. There was no building, they were meeting under the shade of a tree. But, when they started singing and praising the Lord, it was evident that the joy which they had was great. This challenged all of us. Ron and Shirley were impressed at seeing people who had no material goods, and yet had such joy. It made them cry. Ron gave a word of encouragement to the church.

After that, we went back to Kampala. Ron and Shirley stayed the whole three months and faithfully ministered to those first believers in Seguku. We did not know at that time that the Lord had started a work which was going to touch thousands in the years ahead. And, for me, I didn't know that the Lord had given us a man with whom we were going to work with together for many years to come.

It has now been over fifteen years, and Ron and Shirley are going on with God's work. They have worked hard to tell the Americans how good Uganda is, and a good place to visit. As I write, hundreds have now visited our mission and we have a number of missionaries who are working with us.

Ron and Shirley DeVore founded World Outreach Ministry Foundation. This ministry is doing more than I could have ever imagined.

We have planted churches and built schools. We are reaching out to more than twenty prisons and we are also helping orphans and widows. We have set up Bible Schools in Kampala and Masaka. Each month we conduct crusades. We are able to do these things through the efforts of Ron and Shirley DeVore. A country which they came to visit for a short stay, over fifteen years ago, became their home. Now, in their sixties, they are still going strong. They have been a wonderful encouragement to me, our mission, and our country.

~*~*~

A DIVINE APPOINTMENT

God is not a man, that He should lie,
Nor the son of man, that He should repent.
Has He said, and will He not do it?
Or has He spoken, and will He not make it good?
Numbers 23:19

God is not a man that He should lie. Still, in the eleventh chapter of Numbers, the children of Israel complained to Moses because there was no meat for them to eat, only manna. It was very hard on Moses.

So, the Lord said that He was going to give them meat. And this meat would not last only for one or two days, nor five or ten days, but rather for a whole month! This was hard for Moses to believe, but in verse 23, the Lord said to Moses, "Has the Lord's arm been shortened? Now you shall see whether what I say will happen to you or not."

"There are times when God will give a word, but because of the outward circumstances, the situation will look impossible. My Friend, never stay in your unbelief. Believe what the Lord has to say." - Pastor Kaweesa

In the year 2000, I was visiting the U.S.A. Pastor Ron DeVore always invites some of us native pastors from Africa to come and meet the American pastors and Christians who are supporting the work in Africa. During this time when I came, Pastor Murray Jackson of Crusade International in Wisconsin invited me to visit him for two weeks and to meet his people who also help us in Africa.

While on the airplane traveling to be with Pastor Murray, the Lord spoke to me and told me to fast for three days. When I arrived, I told Murray what the Lord had instructed me to do, and he agreed to join me. During our time of prayer, the Lord gave me a vision where I saw myself standing in a very large church speaking. In my mind, I thought that, "Maybe the church Murray is taking me to is a very large church". I had never thought that I would one day stand to speak in the Assembly of God Brownsville Revival in Pensacola, Florida.

I had met many pastors who had gone there to see that great revival. Pastor Steven Mayanga had told me that when he visited that revival, those present from other countries were invited to stand, tell what country they were from, and then share one or two words in their language.

Murray told me that we were to go to visit the Brownsville Revival, and to also see his son who was attending the School of Ministry. I was very happy to hear that! I had desired to visit that place and see what the Lord was doing. But in my mind, it never occurred to me that God could open a door for me and that I would be given time to share about what the Lord has done for the church in Uganda.

The first night we were down there, the Lord spoke to me in a night vision that I would be speaking at the revival and that Murray and I would pray for His people at the meeting. I did not believe that vision. I said, "Lord, I am not one of those big preachers who have big ministries known all over the world. Lord, most of the American pastors who have large churches have never even themselves spoken at that revival. What about me, a poor black preacher?" I went on to tell the Lord how poor my country is that I come from and how some of the pastors of the large churches never allow such a pastor like me to even stand and give a testimony of two minutes.

Everything that I was thinking about the vision was negative. In the morning I asked Pastor Murray if he had ever preached or given a testimony at this revival. He told me, "No."

I said, "Lord, do you see? It is impossible!"

"Let me tell you, my Brother or Sister, what is impossible with man is possible with God. What you cannot do, the Lord can do and even greater than you have ever imagined." - Pastor Kaweesa

That morning we met with a wonderful man of God who was in charge of pastoral care and domestic placement. Murray wanted to find out if he would consider sending some of their students to Africa. His name was D. Keith Collins. As we were getting ready to leave, he wanted us to pray for him, which we did. As we prayed, the Lord gave me a word for him and it was exactly what he had been praying for. He had been asking the Lord to give him a word regarding what he was to do.

After prayer, Keith asked Murray if he would bring me to the revival meeting the next night for me to speak maybe twenty minutes. Murray told him yes. It was like I was daydreaming. Within my heart I started repenting for doubting God.

The night came. It was around 7:30 p.m. and Dr. Brown was conducting the meeting. He invited Keith to come and introduce Murray and I. Murray introduced me to speak to the Christians. It was amazing. I was given one of those great welcomes as any powerful man of God gets.

I spoke about how the Lord protected us during the time of Idi Amin. I used about twenty minutes and was about to sit down when Dr. Brown stood and asked me to give a word from the Lord for America. That was during the time the election was going on for the president in the United States. *(The 2000 Presidential election, Bush and Gore.)* The Lord had given me the word about two weeks before. I went ahead and gave it.

Afterwards, I felt the Spirit of the Lord tell me to pray for America. I told all the Christians to stand and we prayed for the nation for another thirty minutes. The Spirit of God moved in a great way. After that, they asked me and Murray to pray for the people. Most of the people wanted us to lay our hands on them, and we did a few, but could not lay our hands on all the thousands who were there at that time.

~*~*~

"The Lord had done what He had said. God is God, and I am encouraging you, my Brother and Sister, whatever the Lord has spoken about your life, ministry or anything, it will come to pass. Let God be God. Only believe!" - Pastor Kaweesa

THOSE WHO HAVE ENCOURAGED ME

There are certain people who have impacted my life over the years, from the first day that the Lord called me to preach the gospel. Without them, I maybe would not be who I am today.

One of those important people was my Auntie Margaret, who I shared about with you earlier. She was very instrumental in teaching me to pray and seek the face of the Lord. One of the "pillars", one of the things that have made this ministry a success, is prayer and fasting. I have been using them ever since I began the ministry. My Auntie was an instrument of the Lord used to teach and encourage me. I came to realize that those who seek the Lord diligently shall find Him.

I love those who love me,
and those who seek me
diligently will find me.
Proverbs 8:17

I stood on the scriptures. The fasting of my Auntie and myself has really helped me throughout all the years of hardships, persecutions, killings and troubles. So, I want to let you know that my Auntie Margaret is a wonderful lady. Even now, as I have faced some very big problems that I thought I could not overcome, she has set me down and counseled me. And, the Lord has given me success through her counseling.

~*~*~

Another person who has been instrumental in my life is a pastor, named Peterson. When he saw that the Lord had gifted and anointed me to preach the Gospel, he was very quick to try to guide me. He let me know what I should do and what I should not do. He was very instrumental in encouraging me to grow in the Lord. He has always uplifted me. In the natural I was very shy, but Pastor Peterson saw within me a gift.

I remember one time we had gone to a crusade. He had not notified me that I was going to preach. Eventually, he just called me up after the singing and testimonies. He went forward and introduced that we have a young man of God that has been anointed to preach the Gospel. Then, he announced, "This is Stephen Kaweesa!" I was overwhelmed! You can imagine someone who has not stood before the people, someone who has not stood before the congregation. And here it is announced that I am to preach!

But, I accepted and went forward a bit shaken and trembling. Within me, I heard a voice say, "Go and preach!"

Later, everyone said, "My, this is a preacher!"

So, from that time forward, Pastor Peterson continued to counsel me and encourage me. He gave me books to read. Sitting under his ministry in the early 1970s had a great affect on my life.

~*~*~

Another man of God who encouraged me during the underground times was Mulindwa. He was very gifted in the Word of Knowledge and in the Word of Prophecy. He could also really cast out devils and demons! I admired this man.

I remember one time Mulindwa came with a young man who was deaf and dumb. He explained how he had met this young man. Mulindwa had been traveling on a bus when he met a family. He shared Jesus with them and they accepted Christ and prayed. Mulindwa noticed that their son was not hearing or speaking. He requested that the mother and father allow him to take the young man with him, promising that in a week he would bring their son back to them hearing and speaking.

He came to our church and explained this to us. He was very happy and excited. He told us how God is so good, how Jesus is so wonderful. Mulindwa was thanking Jesus that He was going to heal this young man within the week.

I had just accepted Christ and I looked at that minister and wondered, "How does he know that? How is he so sure? What if the young man does not speak?" I had all those kinds of questions like anyone who doubts the power of God and has not experienced the power of God.

Mulindwa had come to church on a Wednesday evening service. When he returned on Sunday, I tell you, that young man was hearing very, very well. And he was speaking! I was so impressed. I said, "Oh, God, this is what I want. I want to be like this man." I admired him.

Another time that Mulindwa came to visit us, there were about five of us in the living room studying the Bible. He had come from a far journey about one hundred miles away. We were sharing scriptures on the topic concerning love. When he came in one of the brothers said, "This word that we are sharing is very important, very wonderful. Why don't we go back a little bit so that our brother who has just come in can hear this?"

Mulindwa said, "No. You don't need to do that." And he mentioned to each one of us what we had already shared. Then, he said we should continue. I was very, very much impressed. My eyes were so wide open. I wondered how God could use a person in such a way to know things like that.

I said, "God, I must learn from this man."

He had come to our church to fast and pray and to seek the face of the Lord for three days. I told my aunt that I was going to spend some time praying with this preacher, which I did. I wanted to know what kind of secret or special thing he had. What I discovered was that he had the Living Word. Mostly, he shared with me scriptures from the Bible. Also, he prayed with me and prophesied over me how the Lord was going to use me. He told me how I would one day travel to nations around the world and how I was going to help a number of people to come to know Jesus Christ. He really encouraged me.

~*~*~

Also, there have been others who have encouraged me, like the late Mr. and Mrs. Musisi, who gave us their little house to meet in. Even in danger, they risked their lives for the sake of Jesus Christ. They had a great impact on me. Watching them serve, gave me a desire to do my level best to serve my Living God.

~*~*~

Another one who encouraged me was my brother Paul of Kabowa. We were with him underground. When I moved to Seguku to come and work I invited him to join us as we opened the mission. We did not know all that would happen, but he joined us and has been a great support to us these last fifteen years.

~*~*~

There were also ladies in the seventies that forsook their homes, brought their bedding and came right to the church and prayed without ceasing. Those ladies, whom I admire, prayed and prayed and sought the face of the Lord. They prayed through the night, went home, worked, and then came back to the church day after day, month after month, year after year. Those older ladies have been such a great encouragement to me.

~*~*~

Also, Brother Andrew with the Open Doors ministry was a great encouragement to me. It was back in the 1970s when I got in contact with his ministry. Someone had given my name to Brother Andrew and he invited me, along with some other pastors, to come to Nairobi,

Kenya. Of the preachers invited, I was the youngest, only eighteen years old. It was a great encouragement to me during those terrible years of war to know that someone "out there" cared.

It was very difficult for us preachers from Uganda to travel to Kenya during those years. Every time we did, Idi Amin's men were on our backs. But, thank God, we made it. His ministry promised thirty dollars to each one of us, which they sent every month for some good years, I don't remember how many. Also, I was given a bicycle, which was a great blessing! That was the bicycle that Idi Amin's men came and took when I was conducting a night prayer in one of our secret meetings. It was bad, but the Lord used the bicycle to spare our lives. When the soldiers left our place that night, they went to another village and killed a number of people.

The support that Brother Andrew's ministry gave to me during those very difficult years in our country enabled me to reach out to many places with the Gospel of Jesus Christ.

~*~*~

In 1983, I met Reinhard Bonnke in Amsterdam at a great conference. He had invited all of us ministers from Uganda to have a meeting with himself. He explained to us how he wanted to come to Uganda to conduct a crusade. Also, he invited us to come to Harare, Zimbabwe for the Fire Conference in 1984.

As a young Ugandan minister, this was a great encouragement to me. Also, the way Reinhard Bonnke loved our country in such a bad time was very uplifting. He did come to Uganda and spoke to us pastors and ministers. He gave a word of encouragement to us. This made a great impact on my life and my ministry.

Reinhard Bonnke also conducted crusades in our country, and even in the midst of war, people got born-again. Uganda is now going through revival and I am happy to be a part of what God is doing here and in the world.

~*~*~

Another person who was a great encouragement to me was Brother Billy Graham. In 1983, he invited me to come and attend a World Evangelism Conference in Amsterdam, Holland. He paid for my round-trip air ticket, for my hotel and everything.

I, as a young minister, was very blessed as I joined the other 4000 pastors and evangelists. I was so much blessed to sit under Brother Graham's teaching and the teachings of other mighty men and women of God.

To this day, I don't know who gave him my name for the invitation, but what I do know is that the Lord knew that I needed that encouragement. Maybe I was one of the youngest preachers, but the Lord had something more for me in the years ahead.

As I write now, after almost twenty years, the words from that conference are still fresh in my mind. The Lord has blessed my ministry. I have won many souls for Christ, and I have seen the Lord change my country from a country full of witchcraft and unbelief, to a country where revival is going on.

~*~*~

Back in the seventies, T.L. Osborn brought a crusade to Kenya. He sent an invitation for me to attend. Where he got my name, I don't know, maybe I will know when we reach heaven. He provided transportation and accommodation.

That crusade was an eye opener! When I saw such great miracles taking place, me as a young preacher, I said, "Lord, this is what I want!" Although it was very difficult to cross into Kenya from Uganda at that time, I made it and that crusade brought a great change in my ministry.

I had believed in miracles and the Lord was performing miracles in my ministry, however, that crusade was another step to reach more of the Lord and to believe God for greater miracles. God is good. Brother T.L. visited Uganda in the eighties even during such a bad time of war. It was a great encouragement to me.

~*~*~

Morris Cerrulo was also a great encouragement to me in those early years. In 1978, he invited me to attend a minister's conference in Nairobi, Kenya. He promised to pay for everything, which he did. I was only twenty-one, and was so thankful to be a part of God's ministers from all over Africa. Those two months meant a lot to me. I was the youngest of all the ministers who came, numbering over four hundred, but was treated the same.

Idi Amin was still the president then, and for a preacher to travel to Nairobi was one of the most difficult things. I remember how five people were picked from the bus on which I was traveling, and I'm sure they were killed. On the way there, we had to go through sixteen road blocks. At one road block, the soldiers came across my Bible, and they almost wanted to take me to be killed because of my Bible, but the Lord is good, and I made it to the conference.

It was such a great blessing to me, a young preacher, to be seated with Morris Cerrulo and the team he brought. I have never been the same since. It has now been twenty-five years and I have seen God move in many ways.

~*~*~

"ME? WRITE A BOOK?"

Another person who encouraged me was Pastor Jeff Gorman, who helped persuade me to write this book. Always in my heart I had wanted to write what I have gone through during my time of ministry and during the time of persecution. I had the idea of writing a book, and had prayed about it, but did not know how to handle it. I did not know where to begin, it was something beyond my reach.

Here in Uganda, things are very, very expensive. It would only be a dream to write and print a book in Uganda. And, if you could, where would you sell it? Many questions were reeling within my mind, and I thought, "What can I do?" But, the Lord knew the perfect time.

I met Pastor Jeff in Seattle. He invited me to visit his church in Ellensburg and preach, which I did. As I gave a testimony of what we went through during Idi Amin's time, Jeff remembered hearing about me back in the seventies. He had read a story in Brother Andrew's newsletter about when Idi Amin's soldiers had come to kill us, but angels of the Lord intervened and the soldiers ran away. Pastor Jeff was so amazed to actually meet someone he had read about over twenty years ago, and who was now in his church preaching!

After that, he sat me down and requested that I write my testimony. He said that he and his wife would help me write a book. I didn't take them seriously. I returned to Uganda and did nothing about it.

Later, Pastor Jeff came to Uganda and said, "You have to write your testimony." Then, he said, "Okay, what I can do is this. When I return home, I will send a recorder and tapes for you, and then you will just speak those words and we will put them in the form of a book." He sent those things to me and it was a very, very great encouragement to me.

I am brought to tears remembering how God has given me such wonderful people who believed in my ministry and me. As I look back at their commitment of how they have backed me and stood with me, I am very thankful. Each one of us needs people like that.

So, I am thankful for those who have come along to uphold me.

"There are people who have died with their gifts. They have died with their talents. They have died with their knowledge. They have died with their wisdom. Why?

There was no one to encourage them to put their knowledge and wisdom, gifts and talents to use. So, when they died, they died leaving all that useless. It disappeared forever.

My dear Sister and Brother out there, perhaps God is calling you to be an encouragement to someone near you, to your pastor, to the evangelist, to the teacher, to the prophet and the apostle. Maybe God has gifted you. Please do what you are supposed to do. Because when you do, the work of the Living God is going to go on." - Pastor Kaweesa

About the Author

Pastor Kaweesa is a native pastor serving in Uganda, Africa. He has been serving nearly thirty years founding churches, conducting crusades, teaching in Bible Schools, as well as caring for orphans and prisoners. He is the Vice-Chairman of Uganda Christian Outreach Ministries and the Co-Pastor of Seguku Worship Center. He is a well respected spiritual leader in his home country. The fruit of his life truly exemplifies that of a faithful servant of his Lord Jesus Christ.

HOW TO CONTACT PASTOR KAWEESA

PASTOR STEPHEN KAWEESA
c/o W.O.M.F.
P. O. BOX 23267
FEDERAL WAY, WA 98093-0267

TO ORDER ADDITIONAL COPIES OF THIS BOOK
DIRECTLY FROM THE PUBLISHER,
PLEASE LOG ON TO www.1stbooks.com

OR CONTACT:

G.R.O.C.
P.O. BOX 879
ELLENSBURG, WA 98926

OR CALL 509/ 933-2500

OR VISIT www.greatroundup.org

Printed in the United States
124322LV00006B/25-93/A

9 781410 719898